Common Ground

A Gathering of Poems on Rural Life

Edited by Mark Vinz and Thom Tammaro

Dacotah Territory Press, 1989

A Note on the Second Printing: Aside from the correction of a very few typographical errors and the restoration of one lost line of poetry, the text of this edition remains the same as that of the first. The only other changes are in the book's cover. The original subtitle, *A Gathering of Poets from the 1986 Marshall Festival,* has been replaced with *A Gathering of Poems on Rural Life,* a clearer description of the book's contents; the color of the cover has also been changed to reflect the editors' original intentions (inadvertently changed during printing), and quotations from two reviews replace Mary Ann Grossman's descriptive comments on the Marshall festival.

ISBN: 0-941127-04-4

Copyright © 1988 by Dacotah Territory Press
2nd printing, 1989.

Dacotah Territory Press
P.O. Box 931
Moorhead, MN 56560

Printed in the United States of America

Cover photograph: "North of Regent, North Dakota"
                      Wayne Gudmundson
Interior photograph: "Sheyenne Valley, North Dakota"
                      Wayne Gudmundson
Layout: Susan Sand

The editors would like to express their deep appreciation to Tom Sand, St. Paul, Minnesota, for his generous support of this project.

To the Memory of Alec Bond
1938-1985
Poet, Teacher, Friend

"The common day and night—the common earth and waters,
Your farm—your work, trade, occupation,
The democratic wisdom underneath, like solid ground for all."

--Walt Whitman

Contents

What We Didn't Know We Knew

We have long wanted to put together an anthology of contemporary Midwestern poetry—partly because it has been more than ten years since the publication of volume two of Lucien Stryk's *Heartland: Poets of the Midwest*, and partly because of our own sense of the talent and richness reflected in contemporary Midwestern poetry which has continued to grow during those years. But the problem has always been one of scope and magnitude. There are so many strong writers throughout the Midwest today—how could we ever edit a book that includes everyone who deserves to be in it? Well, the Marshall Festival of 1986 helped solve some of those logistical problems and provided us with a splendid opportunity and impetus. Here was a gathering that, while not exclusively Midwestern, included over thirty Midwestern poets. And while such a writers' festival will always be limited in one way or another, here at least was a means for us of defining a selection process. Certainly, there are numerous omissions—but there are also many writers here that would be included in *any* anthology of Midwestern poetry or poetry which celebrates the rural. Our goal, then, has been to offer a representative sampling, not an inclusive one, and record of a particular Midwestern event that also goes far beyond that particular time and place. That, we think, is as much as any anthologists can hope to accomplish.

The nature of the anthology itself is bound to the usual issues concerning "regionalism." And while much has been written in defense of and as a challenge to the idea of "regionalism," we raise the issue not so much out of our need to settle it once and for all, but rather to clarify and make public our own feelings about regionalism and to offer a perspective which we hope will diffuse the issue for more useful purposes.

In her wonderful little pamphlet on Richard Hugo in the "Western Writers Series" from Boise State University, Donna Gerstenberger writes that the term "'regional poet' is too often, in our critical vocabulary, a dismissive term. . .a polite equivalent for 'minor'" and that the term "'regionalist' describes as much a way of working with the materials as anything else. . . ." And while Gerstenberger is writing specifically about Hugo, we also feel that she is speaking about regional writers in general.

> To say properly that a writer is a regional writer is not to say
> that he or she is good or bad, limited or universal, accessible or
> unaccessible. It is simply to say that a writer, within degrees,
> goes about the creation of fictional worlds in a certain way.
> Those writers that are 'minor' or 'limited' etc., are not minor
> limited because they are regionalists but because as writers they
> are minor or limited. . . . [Regionalism] is useful as a descriptive
> term but not as a term of value or as a definition of limits.
> (Donna Gerstenberger, *Richard Hugo* [Boise, Idaho: Western
> Writers Series #59, Boise State University, 1983], pp. 39-41).

We wonder, for example, why "regional" as a term of valuation or even as description has never been used in reviews or critical essays about the recent crop of novels and collections of short stories about New York City's subterranean night life, and especially those focusing on contemporary SoHo culture? Certainly, these writers—like many Midwestern writers—employ similar methods to create their fictional world: namely the landscape, the linguistic idioms, and the iconography of their particular region. Yet who thinks of these writers as "regionalists?" Again, to recall Gerstenberger, these writers are simply "[going] about creating their fictional worlds in a certain way." We hope our readers will keep this in mind as they read their way through the poems in this anthology. For ultimately the success or failure of the poems herein must be measured by their success or failure as poems, as works of art possessing their own integrity. We believe the poets represented here would expect and demand nothing less.

What we hope this anthology accomplishes, then, is a reaffirmation of several things, but of three in particular. First is *that positive and enduring sense of the regional*: that American literature has always been rooted in particular places and that its best writers have consistently explored the richness of their own places and experiences for that necessary link between particular and universal, local and international, regardless of whether it be Hannibal, Missouri, or the East Village in New York. Second, we hope these pages indicate that Midwestern poetry is indeed very much alive and well today, even if its audience in the Midwest sometimes tends to forsake it for some vague sense of "national" emanating from either coast. Third, while we will indeed find some common themes in these poems—a common sense of Midwestern iconography and idiom—we will also find much diversity in voice and emphasis as well as many surprises. Our goal, as that of the Marshall Festival itself, has been to focus on the rural Midwest, yet even within these limits these poets have a wonderful facility for showing us with freshness what we tend to overlook or take for granted. Poetry, finally, has much to do with *seeing*, and with being *able* to see. What all these writers know so well is that poetry doesn't spring simply from the exotic and the remote; it is right here, all around us.

Finally, another principle which guided us in our selection process has been to choose poems which we hope are accessible to a variety of readers, but especially to students. We have both drawn heavily upon Midwestern writing in our teaching; we have both experienced the excitement of seeing young Midwesterners discover (to paraphrase Robert Frost) what they didn't know they knew—about their place, their backgrounds, their imaginations, and the rich heritage and continuing changes of which we are all a part.

It is with a renewed sense of gratitude, then, to Phil Dacey and all who worked so hard to create the Marshall Festival that we present this anthology—one which we hope will help to bring about others, and one which we also hope will lead us to celebrate that *seeing* which is so vital to poetry and place alike.

Mark Vinz
Thom Tammaro
Moorhead, Minnesota

A Long Road Without Inns

Given the origin of the idea of festival in the *rus*, or countryside, a writers' festival necessarily carries with it a reference to the rural, whereas a writers' conference is always urban, whether held in New York City or Laramie, Wyoming. The earliest festivals were agricultural and religious celebrations. In the classical world, big-city politicians seeking to aggrandize their power eventually appropriated such popular celebrations, subtly but significantly changing them in the process. Participants in *The Marshall Festival: A Celebration of Rural Writers and Writing* (Southwest State University, Marshall, Minnesota, May 5 through 9, 1986) testified to something of the original spirit, through which community was renewed, not managed.

The bright green cover of the program for the festival emphasized that the celebration would include besides the expected poetry and fiction "Music, Dance, Art, Drama, Film." Inside, the program listed more than sixty-five separate events and more than fifty scheduled writers and other artists. The week, with many events necessarily overlapping, was by design more than any one person could experience. The image of a cornucopia, although never explicitly employed in the promotion of the festival, was present both subliminally and in informal talk before, during, and after the festival, acting as a reminder of the roots of festival and of the miles of farmland spreading in all directions from around the site of this particular gathering.

The immediate precedent for the festival was the 1978 *Minnesota Writers' Festival*, also hosted by Southwest State University and also a week-long gathering. The response to that festival, which by its last day, according to novelist Frederick Manfred, "took on the aspects of an artistic firestorm," planted the seed for another such venture after a suitable period of time. That the eight-year lapse between these festivals should have been one of the standard intervals of time between ancient festivals was, as far as anyone can prove, coincidental. The festival that initiated this anthology, unlike its predecessor, drew from throughout the United States for much of its personnel, used the rubric "rural" as a guide in achieving a significant shape, and surpassed its model in variety and abundance.

A less direct precedent, but one deserving credit, was *The Gathering*, which was held in St. Peter, Minnesota, from August 9 through 16, 1981, and sponsored by Cherry Creek Theatre. Its staff, while comprising men and women primarily committed to work in the theatre, brought to the design and execution of the week a broad vision. *The Gathering* generally asked the question, "How can we act better on stage and in the world?" The crossover of personnel between the two festivals was small (McGrath, LeSueur, the Paddocks, perhaps a few others); the crossover of planners between the two was nonexistent. Yet the generous and lingering spirit of *The Gathering* called for a gesture in response. No doubt many appropriate gestures followed upon it, partially created by it; *The Marshall Festival* was probably one of them.

The festival can also be traced back to an early chairman of the host institution's English department, Dr. Delbert Wylder. Believing the division in so many English departments between writers and scholars to be unfortunate and unreasonable and that writers ought to enjoy a position of centrality rather than marginality in their departments, he followed as often as possible a policy of hiring writers as faculty. The result was the creation of a long-lasting matrix unusually conducive to writers. Out of it, fifteen or so years later, came *The Marshall Festival*, an undertaking of such scope that only a story of considerable preliminary groundwork of the sorts described above could properly explain it.*

Although the distinction in the festival's sub-title between writers and writing was cumbersome, it served the purpose of defining complementary emphases at the festival: on writers who, no matter where they live, write about the rural, and writers who are long-term rural residents but who may not focus on the rural in their work. Thus Amy Clampitt, who makes her home in New York City, was invited on the strength of her poetry about the natural world and her rural upbringing in Iowa, while Robert Bly, who has certainly written poems with rural images but whose focus has been on spiritual and psychological issues having less to do with place than universal human nature, was invited because rural Minnesota has always been his home. Wendell Berry combines rural residence and rural subject matter. Among the writers invited who were not able to attend were N. Scott Momaday, James Welch, Mary Oliver, and Louise Erdrich. Poets were heavily represented among the festival's personnel but they were matched by an equal or greater number of novelists, short story writers, essayists, journalists, editors, painters, musicians, actors, a naturalist, and a dancer.

By definition, the fruits of a cornucopia are beyond accounting, and each participant in the festival, whether scheduled personnel or member of the audience (which latter came from at least five midwestern states besides Minnesota), had his or her own list of highlights, but some sampling of special happenings is surely in order: Carol Bly and Donald Hall holding a "Conversation Between Old Friends" as they reminisced about their literary and personal connections over the years; Robert Bly, Frederick Manfred, and Thomas McGrath free-wheeling together in response to the question, "What Keeps Us Here and Going?"; Bill Holm, called by Ted Kooser in *Coda* "one of Minnesota's few national treasures," tuxedoed and romping on piano between readings of his poems about boxelder bugs; Hungarian-born dancer Gustav Fogarrasy improvising spell-binding modern dances to poems by Leo Dangel and others, read by the poets themselves; Thomas McGrath introducing and answering questions after the showing of *The*

---

*There would, of course, be nothing to explain if the following groups had not provided funds to support the festival, which required two years of planning: The Bremer Foundation, The Bush Foundation, Southwest Minnesota Arts & Humanities Council, and, at Southwest State University, the Rural Studies Program and the departments of Adult and Continuing Education and English.

Museum and the Fury, a rarely-seen documentary about the Holocaust, scripted by McGrath in the fifties for the Polish government; Carol Bly eloquently half-repeating from memory and half-improvising an hour-long short story before an amazed audience; satirical song-writer from Montana Greg Keeler, accompanied by his own raucous and subtle guitar, singing his work before a large, enthusiastic crowd that would not let him quit; the then-president of the university and now Chancellor of the State University System, Robert Carothers, doing what probably no other college president in the United States could do—concluding the on-campus proceedings with a poetry reading of his own work that matched or exceeded in substance and performance any other reading given that week in a week of extraordinary readings; Dave Etter bringing to life the title poem of his book *Live at the Silver Dollar* by indeed reading live to a packed house at the Silver Dollar in Ghent, the first bar west of the Mississippi to open after Prohibition; and the ad hoc formation, in a lounge at Southwest State University, of a temporary bookstore that, by stocking publications of all the scheduled writers, became, for that week, the most interesting bookstore in the southwestern quarter of Minnesota.

A perusal of the complete schedule reveals the unavoidable inadequacy of any such list of highlights. For examples, Wendell Berry brought to every appearance his special blend of passion and intelligence, and the unfailing youthfulness of Meridel LeSueur shone throughout her stay at the festival. Nor can any schedule reflect events like Bill Kloefkorn's spontaneous selection, by a female segment of the audience, as Sexiest Man at the Festival, an honor that perhaps confirms the justice of his earlier formal selection by Nebraska as her State Poet.

When the festival was over, large claims were made for it. Mary Ann Grossman in the *St. Paul Pioneer Press-Dispatch* wrote that "it seems unlikely such a stellar group of men and women of letters will ever be gathered in one place in the state again." Jack Miller, the editor of *North Country Anvil* (Millville, Minnesota) said the festival represented "an inspiring vision for the culture of literature—and the ability to help bring that vision to realization." Paul Gruchow (*Journal of a Prairie Year*) said he felt he could write for a year off the energy he got from it and that what the festival accomplished was "exactly what great universities are supposed to be doing." Their comments represent countless others.

One might ask, What good is such a festival? The comments above suggest what could be the ideal answer. The gathering of "stellar men and women" is not an end in itself, though it can provide a party-atmosphere. But if those men and women help to establish—or at least point to the possibility of the establishment of—a context or community in which the individual can flourish, a culture that acts as a source of energy for a creative person, then such a festival probably has its justification. Almost certainly the positive effects of such a festival are not measurable, not even definable. Faith and feeling have to provide some knowledge of the results. The book you are holding in your hand at this moment, of course, is a palpable result of the festival, but the poems that follow this introduction throw us back into the same problem: What good is a poem? The process of answering it would probably follow along the lines taken to answer the question at the start of this paragraph.

Democritus (c. 400 B.C.) summed up his opinion of festival in one line: "Life without festivals is a long road without inns." Inns refresh, renew, provide a place for nourishment and sleep. Because of the demands of the festival, sleep was at a premium that week. Yet many people felt they had fallen into a good dream. Ted Kooser wrote an article for *Coda* (November/December 1986) entitled "The Marshall Festival: Good Spirits Under the Comet's Tail" (this was the time of Halley). His concluding description of the festival suggests the quality of dream many people felt:

> It is said that there are certain spots on the globe where magical lines intersect and wonderful things occur. Southern Minnesota does, after all, include the Bly farm at Madison, where once so many important moments for contemporary poetry were passed, and Pine Island, where the shadow of James Wright's hammock still lies on the grass.

> At Marshall I was struck again and again by the friendliness, the generosity, and the lack of competition between the writers. I have never seen a group of people so happy to see one another. Emilie Buchwald called the festival "a glorious collision of people." Somebody speculated that it might have been dust from the comet's tail that made for all the harmony and goodwill, but I contend that it was the common Minnesota dust on every shoe.

By remarking offhandedly after the publication of the *Coda* article that it was a piece of journalistic "fluff," Kooser acknowledged the unreality of all dream. Yet, as the hardly rural Marianne Moore told us, there can be "real toads in imaginary gardens." It is the component of truth in dreams, not their component of unreality, that is always of interest. The enthusiastic celebrants at The Marshall Festival chose to believe in the truth of the dream it was.

Philip Dacey
Professor of English, Southwest State
University
Director, The Marshall Festival

Common Ground

Joseph Amato

BROR ANDERSON'S BIRDS

In the spring of what Bror knew to be the last year of
  his life,
He put six goslings on his pond.
He took joy in their growth.

And he spoke to everyone of their certain flight
And possible return.
Their migration became his last parable.

And I, for one, will look for the signs of Bror,
Not in a cemetery, amidst marble inscriptions,
But in the spring, near the horizon,
On the edge of every bird's wing.

A WINTER PEACE DANCE

God is cold,
And I am lost along the road again.
For the last twelve years I kept getting lost.
My blue eyes grow paler all the time,
Losing hold of what they see.

I am in front of this farm house;
I am walking around it—swirling like the snow—
Seeing the house and not seeing it:
Its light, this snow, my loss.

They guide me in as if I am a blind man;
They talk nice, they offer tea,
And as they phone the highway patrol,
I slip out.

I know too much,
I have thought too long,
I have felt too strongly,
And been lost too often
To be found again.

I'll sleep out,
And when I awake on that hard, frozen earth
I'll dance my last dance,
I'll embrace the prairie winds,
I'll dance the winter I have been,
I'll finish the winter I suffer.

No voices, no bands, no houses.
Cold and moonlight in a crystal silence
Too cold for any howling dog,
My dance,
And winter peace.

4

Wendell Berry

THE PEACE OF WILD THINGS

When despair for the world grows in me
and I wake in the night at the least sound
in fear of what my life and my children's lives may be,
I go and lie down where the wood drake
rests in his beauty on the water, and the great heron feeds.
I come into the peace of wild things
who do not tax their lives with forethought
of grief. I come into the presence of still water.
And I feel above me the day-blind stars
waiting with their light. For a time
I rest in the grace of the world, and am free.

TO WHAT LISTENS

I come to it again
and again, the thought of the wren
opening his song here
to no human ear—
no woman to look up,
no man to turn his head.
The farm will sink then
from all we have done and said.
Beauty will lie, fold
on fold, upon it. Foreseeing
it so, I cannot withhold
love. But from the height
and distance of foresight,
how well I like it
as it is! The river shining,
the bare trees on the bank,
the house set snug
as a stone in the hill's flank,
the pasture behind it green.
Its songs and loves throb
in my head till like the wren
I sing—to what listens—again.

THE MAN BORN TO FARMING

The grower of trees, the gardener, the man born to farming,
whose hands reach into the ground and sprout,
to him the soil is a divine drug. He enters into death
yearly, and comes back rejoicing. He has seen the light lie down
in the dung heap, and rise again in the corn.
His thought passes along the row ends like a mole.
What miraculous seed has he swallowed
that the unending sentence of his love flows out of his mouth
like a vine clinging in the sunlight, and like water
descending in the dark?

THE WILD GEESE

Horseback on Sunday morning,
harvest over, we taste persimmon
and wild grape, sharp sweet
of summer's end. In time's maze
over the fall fields, we name names
that went west from here, names
that rest on graves. We open
a persimmon seed to find the tree
that stands in promise,
pale, in the seed's marrow.
Geese appear high over us,
pass, and the sky closes. Abandon,
as in love or sleep, holds
them to their way, clear,
in the ancient faith: what we need
is here. And we pray, not
for new earth or heaven, but to be
quiet in heart, and in eye
clear. What we need is here

Robert Bly

DRIVING TOWARD THE LAC QUI PARLE RIVER

I

I am driving; it is dusk; Minnesota.
The stubble field catches the last growth of sun.
The soybeans are breathing on all sides.
Old men are sitting before their houses on carseats
In the small towns. I am happy,
The moon rising above the turkey sheds.

II

The small world of the car
Plunges through the deep fields of the night,
On the road from Willmar to Milan.
This solitude covered with iron
Moves through the fields of night
Penetrated by the noise of crickets.

III

Nearly to Milan, suddenly a small bridge,
And water kneeling in the moonlight.
In small towns the houses are built right on the ground;
The lamplight falls on all fours in the grass.
When I reach the river, the full moon covers it;
A few people are talking low in a boat.

LAZINESS AND SILENCE

I

On a Saturday afternoon in the football season,
I lie in a bed near the lake,
And dream of moles with golden wings.

While the depth of the water trembles on the ceiling,
Like the tail of an enraged bird,
I watch the dust floating above the bed, content.

I think of ships leaving lonely harbors,
Dolphins playing far at sea,
Fish with the faces of old men come in from a blizzard.

II

A dream of moles with golden wings
Is not so bad; it is like imagining
Waterfalls of stone deep in mountains,
Or a wing flying alone beneath the earth.

I know that far out in the Minnesota lake
Fish are nosing the mouths of cold springs,
Whose water causes ripples in the sleeping sand,
Like a spirit moving in a body.

It is Saturday afternoon. Crowds are gathered,
Warmed by the sun, and the pure air.
I thought of this strange mole this morning,
After sleeping all night by the lake.

SNOWFALL IN THE AFTERNOON

I

The grass is half-covered with snow.
It was the sort of snowfall that starts in late afternoon,
And now the little houses of the grass are growing dark.

II

If I reached my hands down, near the earth,
I could take handfuls of darkness!
A darkness was always there, which we never noticed.

III

As the snow grows heavier, the cornstalks fade farther away,
And the barn moves nearer to the house.
The barn moves all alone in the growing storm.

IV

The barn is full of corn, and moving toward us now,
Like a hulk blown toward us in a storm at sea;
All the sailors on deck have been blind for many years.

SITTING WITH MY MOTHER AND FATHER

My father's hard
breathing
we all three
notice.
To continue
to live
here
one must
take air.
Taking air
commits us
to sharing
air with the puma
and the eagle.
But when
breathing stops
he will escape
into the world
without forest
or peak.
He came from
the water world
and does not
want to change
again.
My mother
is not sure
where she
wants to be,
but this
air
world
is all
she can
remember,
and neighbors
are here,
nieces,
nephews,
grandchildren.
She sits
with puzzled eyes
as if to say,
where is the reckless
man who took

me from my father,
Is it this man
with gaunt cheeks
on the bed?
All those times
I drove to town
carefully
on packed snow,
is this what
it comes
to?
Yes, it is,
my dear
mother,
the tablecloths
you saved
are all gone,
the baked corn dish
you made for
your boys,
the Christmas
Eves, opening
gifts of perfume
from your husband,
they are all gone.
The nurses take
my father
for his bath.
"What sort
of flowers
are those?"
"Daisies,"
I say.
A few minutes
later you
ask again.
You and I wait
here for
Jacob
to come back
from his bath.
What can I do
but feel
time
go through me
and sit
with you?

MY FATHER AT 85

His large ears hear
everything.
He listens,
and a hermit
wakes and sleeps
in the hut underneath
his gaunt cheeks.
His eyes blue,
alert,
disappointed
and suspicious
complain
I do not bring him
the nurse's jokes.
He is a small bird
waiting to
be fed,
mostly beak,
an eagle or vulture
or the Pharoah's
servant
just before death.
My arm
on the bed
rests
relaxed
with new love.
All I know
of the Troubadors
I bring
to this bed.
I do not
want or need
to be shamed
by him
any longer.
The general of shame
has dis-
charged him,
and left him
in this small
provincial Egyptian town.
If I do not
wish

to shame him,
then why
not love him?
His long
hands, large, veined,
capable, can
still retain
or hold what he wants.
But is that
what he desired?
Some powerful
engine of desire
keeps on running
inside him.
He never phrased
what he desired,
and I
am his son.

THE POTATO

The potato reminds one of an alert desert stone. It belongs to a race
that writes novels of inspired defeat. It does not move on its own, and
yet there is motion in its shape, as if a whirlwind paused, then turned
into potato flesh when a ghost spit at it. Its skin mottles in places;
potato cities are scattered here and there over the planet. In some
places papery flakes lift off, light as fog that lifts from early morning
lakes.

Despite all its eyes, it's likely that little light gets through. On the
inside the potato is a weighty, meaty thing, heavy as an obsession or a
bear after crossing a river. The odor is damp and cheerful at the same
time. The tongue and the teeth are astonished when they bite into the
raw flesh: "I could never have imagined it," as when the wind falls
and the runner leans forward. The tongue says to the teeth: "I expected
so much plot and there is almost none."

William Boggs

COUNTRY TOWN LOVE STORY

Another disturbance at the Stratton house.
One of the sisters has attempted suicide
For the third time this spring. They seem
To take turns, one cared for and one giving care.

The neighborhood gathers in the red
Slash of ambulance lights to see which
One the paramedics carry out mouth to mouth.
Someone says the doctor is to blame,
Always giving them the pills when he knows
That sooner or later he'll be pumping one
Of their stomachs while the other sister
Cries to take her home for some decent care.

They have been doing this as long
As I can remember. The old people
Say the girls' father was the cause,
Chasing away the young men who came
Courting. He kept the beautiful black-haired
School girls to himself, telling
Them that he would get old
And they must care for him. When I die,
He said, then you can do anything
You want. But your mother died and left me
To get old alone, and it's your duty.

The father's rage and razor strop
Drove love away, and the girls' devotion
Frustrated men. They took other wives.

The old man would not die until ninety-seven,
Leaving behind two grey women
With fat faces who seldom talked.
Now, they've promised to take care
Of each other. They take turns falling
Unconscious into the arms
Of the ambulance crew,
A couple of old crazies dying for love.

RED TAIL

I remember my mother's story
About the hawk she almost killed
When she was nine or ten years old.

She tells how she and two
Of my now white-haired feeble aunts
Did it without calling the men
Or sending someone to fetch a gun.

She remembers her white-haired father
Setting the steel-jawed trap, nailing
The chain to the tall gatepost
Where the chicken hawk would roost
When he came to hunt his easy prey.

She remembers the men taking
The team to the far field
To seed oats that day,
And the hawk hanging alone up high,
Waiting for the men to go so he
Could come in to make his kill,
Knowing only the men handled the guns.

He came in to land on the post
And wait for the hens to leave
Their house, cried, surprised at cold
Cutting steel burning to his bone.

They could not leave him there,
Flapping wildly to fly away,
Being jerked back each time he tried.
Maybe to cut his foot the rest
Of the way off, escaping alive and hurt.

So they picked up a stick
To use as a club and went
To him flying at the chain's end,
Screaming, thrashing the air.
Trying to tear anything free.

The bird was too wild so one sister
Went behind him while the other two
Danced in front and called to him,
Turned his head to take the blow and then
He fell limp and dead against the post.

The bird dead, they pulled the trap
Loose from the gatepost and carried him
Back toward the barn. They were proud
Until the bird came back to life,
Doing a death dance in their arms.

15

They clubbed and killed him again
And then twice more on the way.
Battered, he would not die
For these three young girls,
Would not die until their father struck
Him with an axe, driving from
That head all visions of fat hens
And circling skies and posts with steel
Laid open, and two young girls dancing
In front of him, an easy prey.

MORNING

Through the sun's slow rise
A band of orange light sweeps
The kitchen wall, becomes whiter
As the sun clears the eastern ridge.
Sounds of morning: the television
And its bantering news, the frying
Bacon, the electric coffee pot finally
Coming to its daily climax.
The sounds come to us, waking slowly,
Putting on the clothes of day.

We do what we must, feeling
Like horses in the wrong harness,
Getting ready for the drive
Into town, getting ready to do
The things we must do to keep
This life, burying in traffic and talk
A life lived close to life,
Waiting all day for night.

The morning ritual, the obligatory
Order of things, the smell of coffee
Thick through the house, they all greet
Us walking back in from the henhouse,
The brown eggs still warm
In our straw-lined basket.
Different parts of the same life,
Those at either end not knowing
Much of the person at the other
Except at these times, when one becomes
The other in the clear winter sun.

Robert L. Carothers

MUSKRAT

The trick was to trap them in deep water.
 Let them drown themselves.

Yet often, stumbling up our run,
Still sleepy and shivering in the night before
 morning,
My high boots shattering the night's new ice
That glazed the still pools between the bigger
 rocks,
I'd find one in the faint search of my light,
His rich coat smeared with mud and ice,
Twisting in the steel I laid for him,
Praying in his last need that I might accept
The long lamented lamb his father left me,
The splintered bone crying clean and white
His love from the hung matted flesh
 In another night.

 Too late, too late,
For sharp black eyes and long yellowed teeth,
Under my reigning foot in the rushing waters,
The bubbles of those days rising in silence;
 And I looked away, impatient,
 Shivering under the stars.

CHARLIE NO-FACE

In a shack up Crow's Run hollow
Charlie No-Face sleeps the days,
then, coat high and cap low,
he walks the roads til dawn.
Kenneth Taylor has seen him, and Theron Durr.
In the lights of cars his scars flash
like the phantoms of all our dark dreams:
he has said nothing, not curse nor prayer
since flame fat on his face
burned in his brain words not heard
we ran from.

       Summer evenings
we planned to go to him, but never went
Yet I have seen him in Omaha, and
in Kentucky, and once, in fog,
along the Kennebec River in Maine.
In rain he slouches through my mind
and pinned by pain of horror I face that face:
neither question nor answer
but some black fact that lies in us beneath words:
the hush of snow, a whimper in wind,
a lone soul on a country road.

MY BROTHER

My brother, now rich and comfortable
as a psychiatrist in Portland,
married to the daughter of the President
of The Associates (nice people with money),
once played baseball (left field) with me
in a country ball game in a new-mowed hay field.
I watched him chase a ball to his right,
hands above his head, and stagger slowly sideways
past the ball, on over the edge of a hill, out of sight.
When I got to him he was a strange dance
in the grass, eyes rolled back
as if he saw another, inner world,
and, shocked by what he saw, shook with pale terror.

Later, at a grange fair, he did it again,
this time falling under a cow who,
confused, stepped on his chest.
I, fifteen or sixteen, lifted the cow
off him by myself. When he came back,
he said he had just seen God
who could not speak but sat sobbing
in a worn wooden rocking chair.

I have just called my brother long distance
at his office and he says none of this happened.

HUNT POEM

"At length did cross an Albatross,
Through the fog it came."

Hunting in the grey rain
I came up through the orchard
without hope,
through brush and crab apple in the rain.

A shadow crosses left to right,
not pheasant nor grouse
but some bird out of place,
dark and come at the appointed hour
to coil the limp heart tight.
Heavy with dread I climb over the hill
and cast hard about for signs. Nothing.
Then, from dry and spare stalk of weeds
the form focuses for me,
gaunt ghost of other lives, phantom
great blue heron bird, looking straight
at me, who I am this wet morning
out at the edge of myself.

Oh Bird, I knew you then,
and while you watched with grim calm
I gripped my long gun, thinking
for a quick moment to blast you
out of the world once and for all,
turn mystery to a hump
of grey feathers and too long legs lost
to grace and eerie poise.
But that is too much for a man to dare,
and you turn and go slowly
in incredible flight, great
dipping wings west and east,
neck tucked back, up and over
three quivering oaks against the sky.

Gone, I want you out of my mind too.
But along the highway later and
out of my office window you cross
from cloud to cloud and behind the dark moon
bless and curse, curse and bless
my trembling life,
saying, crying, There is no forgiveness,
none, never, not in the long life,
not in the rains of sorrow,
not, not yet in the empty grave.

20

Amy Clampitt

THE ARROW IN MY MIND

I

Stillness of hoarfrost, the daylight furred
the shedding like some celestial animal;
stillness of snowdrifts lulling with thoughts of burial
in this region of drive-ins and shopping centers,
power lines, reformatory walls.
                          The Santee Sioux
once hunted hereabouts, but in the Moon When Deer
Shed Their Horns, seventeen hundred of them, mostly
women and children, were shunted, a four-miles-long
procession, into a fenced enclosure at Fort Snelling
while their fate was decided. "Exterminate or banish!"
was the cry of the land-hungry settlers, who saw off
the first shipment with shouts of derision and
showers of hurled stones.
                      Dee Brown wrote that down;
I read the book on the bus. The young black I sat next to
between Detroit and Chicago, seeing it, smiled for the first time:
"I read that," he said; "it's a good one." After Chicago,
stop by stop the black faces dwindled. Just before sunrise,
Wisconsin hibernating under a scrim of white, the moon rose too—
a whisper crescent that dissolved with daylight.

The Santee thought moons, the way we think deadlines
and paychecks: Moons of Red Lilies, Chokecherries,
Falling Leaves; Moons of Ponies Shedding, Geese Going,
and Strong Cold. But living from moon to moon,
harvesting elderberries and hickory nuts, attuned
to the seasonal ways of deer and migratory birds,
they had no feeling for progress, lacked a standing army,
and thus were economically unviable—in other words,
not acquisitive enough. So they had to go.

II

Progress. Accumulation of capital. Hence avarice
must be our god for a little longer. Lord Keynes
said that; I found it in a book I carry these days
to read on the subway or while standing in line at the bank
with little old persons who have to manage somehow
on food stamps and Social Security: Avarice, usury
and precaution must be our gods until everyone is rich.

He made that statement forty years ago. The Depression
was on, and the realest thing in the world was Money.
I'm not young any more. I remember. We were poor.

Was that why the prairie seemed so inhospitable—
mud roads, barbed-wire enclosures for the animals,
burdocks in the yard, the windmill pumping,
a mean clapboard house, and in the distance
the lost little towns hunched down like fugitives?

Toward sundown, southbound out of Minneapolis—
one blood-red eyeball huge as a mirror lake
at the world's edge—through territory the Winnebago,
the Pottawattamie, the Sac, the Fox, and others of the Sioux
once inhabited, the thought entered my mind
and would not go, but lodged there hurting like an arrow:
So that was why the prairie never felt like home:
it was stolen! These fields, these farms, these little towns
all stolen Territory! The Winnebago, the Pottawattamie,
the Sac, the Fox, the Sioux are names of counties now,
and no one cares or can afford to think of why.
                                        "The country
was made without lines of demarcation; and it is no man's
business to divide it. Perhaps you think the Creator
sent you here to dispose of it as you see fit. Do not
misunderstand me. I never said the land was mine
to do with as I chose. The one who has the right
to dispose of it is the one who created it." The words
are Chief Joseph's of the Nez Perce, who surrendered
because he had no standing army, and who died
a captive. He said as he handed over his gun,
"I am tired of fighting. Our chiefs are killed.
It is cold and we have no blankets. The little children
are freezing to death. Hear me, my chiefs! I am tired;
my heart is sick and sad. From where the sun now stands
I will fight no more forever."
                                        The sun went down
at a quarter of five in the afternoon, and the arrow
that had torn its way into my mind still lodged there, quivering.

III

Suddenly, everything is revisionary; suddenly
everything I look at is contaminated; shame,
no longer a hidden canker of the ego, becomes
a public thing, lodged in the environment like DDT.
Inherited avarice paves all thoroughfares; the cities
are made of it; the law's foundations are paved out of it,
our well-being plowed from it, from the unbearable
sorrow of the uprooted.

When I think of roots
I think of waterlilies, their floating purity
anchored in muck, and of the people, clearly foreign born,
I saw once in a bus terminal, carrying an uprooted
sheaf of them, each limp bud shut tight
as a dead girl's eyelids. The sorrow of the uprooted:
starved out, bombed out, phased out, hunted down,
deported—all in the name of Progress, by history's engines.
Propelled by those same engines, and by a niggling
discontent, I climbed a little way above the ruck
to look out as a mapmaker would on the conquered
terrain I grew up in—a terrain from which there is
no seceding, no going back to start over, living
on elderberries and hickory nuts, even if I wanted to.
Of course not. It makes no difference that all I wanted
was a little space to be free in, to enjoy the view
of where I came from, to understand what I could
of that wrinkled cuneiform—trade routes and salt licks,
the frayed interweave of watersheds and genealogy—so many
sad wheelbarrows trundling upward
to nowhere but the cemetery.
                              Progress. Enlightment.
Uprooting. The arrow in my mind.
Not what they said I'd find.

WITNESS

An ordinary evening in Wisconsin
seen from a Greyhound bus—mute aisles
of merchandise the sole inhabitants
of the half-darkened Five and Ten,

the tables of the single lit cafe awash
with unarticulated pathos, the surface membrane
of the inadvertently transparent instant
when no one is looking: outside town

the barns, their red gone dark with sundown,
withhold the shudder of a warped terrain—
the castle rocks above, tree-clogged ravines
already submarine with nightfall, flocks

(like dark sheep) of toehold junipers,
the lucent arms of birches: purity
without a mirror, other than a mind bound
elsewhere, to tell it how it looks.

Philip Dacey

THE BLIZZARD

He was a visitor, from the South,
and stuck at the farmhouse like the rest of us.
We'd told him, Don't go out there,
you think you know what it is and what it can do
but you don't,
but he insisted on going for a walk.
Now he was back inside, a snowman there before us,
and as he melted and shed his stiff clothing, he spoke.

"God is a blizzard, I know it now. That's the simple truth.
He's out there for anyone who wants to meet him.
And he's beautiful in his fierce way.
I mean it is a mask he wears, and hides behind,
but that we know him by the mask.
I'm going to move up here and never leave.
If it's good enough for God it's good enough for me.
Yes, you needn't say it,
I know people are getting lost out there in that,
but that's my point. It is something for our
selves to get lost in.
Oh, you look at me funny and I don't blame you.
But let me tell you, out there
there is a whiteness that is more than white.
As a child I was told black is the absence of all color
and white is the presence of all color,
color waiting to be broken up
into rainbow-revelation,
but now I say white is the presence
of Presence,
of what is and what wants you to come in to it and be, too.

"No, don't worry,
I'm not going back and never returning.
I'll have that drink of Scotch:
that's enough being for me at the moment;
I am no saint, though I would like to be.
But I swear by all that is cold,
by all that loves with white intensity,
that this is now my land,
that I will set up house here
and raise a storm of children
who will love storms
and what they are,
and that when I die here
it will be a kind of going blind in the snow,
a going blind from having seen too much."

24

We told him we had lived here all our lives
and there was nothing new he could tell us,
but that he was welcome, if he chose to stay.

PICKING ROCK
—*for Joe and Marcella Matthys*

Renters pick fast and loose;
if you own the land, you pick close.

You can pick a field clean one year,
come back the next, and find more.

They rise up from somewhere far below.
Just how far, I don't know.

It's a rain,
but slow, and upside down.

The higher up you get,
like this tractor seat,
the easier they are to spot.

Sometimes I think there are
pregnant ones down there.

Most are granite, some are limestone.
This is no work for one person alone.

There's one kind, blue-black,
that's twice as heavy as it looks.

This one looks like a brain.
Somebody was thinking too hard again.

Here's an old Indian hammerhead.
You can see where the leather strap fitted.

Sometimes it seems everywhere you look
there's a rock.

THE VOICES

The voices came
when I was eight.
High, whiney voices
of men whose faces I imagined
were small and pinched.
They chattered fast:
I never understood a word.

They'd come unexpectedly
like a summer storm
and I'd cry and run
trembling to my mother.
She couldn't help.
My father said something
about too much reading.

Our family doctor
admitted it was strange
but said he knew the cure:
one teaspoonful
of warm glycerine
in each ear
to drown the men.

So it was done.
When the voices rose
out of the dark of my ear,
when the disembodied souls
swarmed my head
like Satanic gnats
out to get me,

I'd lie on my side,
tearful and afraid,
while my mother tilted
sweet glycerine
warmed at the stove
into the bell of my ear.
Something worked:

the voices slid
slowly beneath the syrup,
sounding betrayed,
like figures in a mist
waving goodbye.
When I was nine,
silence came to live in my ear.

It lives there now.
It lets me sleep.
But when I do I dream
of lost messages,
of bottles floating
to shore and breaking,
their notes escaping as fish

beautifully untranslatable.

STORM

Fish at the hole
Cut wide in ice
Seem to shiver, stunned
At the sight of snow.

The water loses it
Immediately
But there is no end
To the soft flood.

The fish dive
In disbelief, return
And find it true,
The flakes growing even

Larger, filling
Their unblinking eyes.
Slowly their mouths
Open and shut,

Breathing nothing
Translatable about
This whiteness broken
So beautifully in air.

Leo Dangel

GATHERING STRENGTH

I looked over my shoulder
at the bedroom mirror and flexed my biceps.
I inspected my body and studied
the body of Charles Atlas in a comic book.

One time, Old Man Brunner winked
and told me how to build muscles—
every day carry a calf for ten minutes
until it's a cow and you're a gorilla.

In the barn, I bent over the calf,
put my left arm under the neck,
my right arm behind the back legs,
and stood up, the calf across my chest.

I marched in giant steps around the pen.
I dreamed about the people who would come
from all over to watch. The headlines
would say: Boy Carries Full-Grown Steer.

But through the dusty window, I looked
hard at the steers in the feedlot,
their blocky shoulders bumping for space
at the feedbunk. I set the calf down.

NO QUESTION

There was no question,
I had to fight Arnold Gertz
behind the high school that Friday.
All fall he kept throwing pool balls
at me in the rec room.

There was no question,
I was scared spitless at the mere sight
of his grimy fists and bull neck.
When we rolled on the cinders
and grappled and thumped each other,

there was no question,
I was actually winning
when the principal broke us up.
And when Arnold went hunting pheasants
on Sunday, everybody said

there was no question,
he was a damn fool to climb through
a barbed wire fence with a loaded shotgun.
There were exactly eight of us guys
who were classmates of Arnold so

there was no question,
I had to be one of the pall bearers,
even though I never liked Arnold,
never would have, but I was sorry
the accident happened,

there was no question,
and if he hadn't got himself shot,
I wonder if he finally would have let me alone.
There is no question,
I wonder about that.

FARMING THE HIGH SCHOOL HOMECOMING

Okay, let's suppose for a minute
that nothing in the float building
and parade was worth remembering.
And suppose we were
fooling ourselves, thinking
that for once we had something
over the town kids because we
had the flatbed wagons and the chicken wire.
Maybe there was
nothing original in our themes for floats:
a paper heart and a treasure chest
under the words—TIGERS, THE TREASURE
OF OUR HEARTS. Or a boat
mounted on a flatbed—SAILING TO VICTORY.
Or the theme we really wanted,
which the girls vetoed, a giant crepe paper
jock strap—LET THIS NOT BE OUR ONLY SUPPORT.
Suppose there is nothing really important
in all of that, and there probably isn't
(our papier-mache usually crumbled).
Still, we were never in danger
of believing we could cover our plainness
with ceremony and tin foil.
The warm October wind
always whipped in from the country and blew
the pastel Kleenexes clean
out of the chicken wire, exposing
old manure stains on the flatbed tires.

THE AUCTION

Not even a bid
on the old plow
rusting in the grove.

We were married only months
when he took all our money
and bought that plow—

really all my money, money
I had earned as a hired girl,
babysitting, walking beans.

He didn't ask me,
just bought the plow.
Our first big fight.

His main fault maybe—
if something needed doing,
he didn't think about feelings.

I feel him behind me now.
He touches my shoulders in a way
that says he remembers

how much that plow cost.

AFTER FORTY YEARS OF MARRIAGE, SHE TRIES A NEW RECIPE FOR HAMBURGER HOT DISH

"How did you like it?" she asked.

"It's all right," he said.

"This is the third time I cooked
it this way. Why can't you
ever say if you like something?"

"Well if I didn't like it, I
wouldn't eat it," he said.

"You never can say anything
I cook tastes good."

"I don't know why all the time
you think I have to say it's good.
I eat it, don't I?"

"I don't think you have to say
all the time it's good, but once
in awhile you could say
you like it."

"It's all right," he said.

HOW TO TAKE A WALK

This is farming country.
The neighbors will believe
you are crazy
if you take a walk
just to think and be alone.
So carry a shotgun
and walk the fence line.
Pretend you are hunting
and your walking will not
arouse suspicion.
But don't forget
to load the shotgun.
They will know
if your gun is empty.
Stop occasionally.
Cock your head and listen
to the doves you never see.
Part the tall weeds
with your hand and inspect
the ground.
Sniff the air as a hunter would.
(That wonderful smell
of sweet clover is a bonus.)
Soon you will forget
the gun in your hands,
but remember, someone
may be watching.
If you hear beating wings
and see the bronze flash
of something flying up,
you will have to shoot it.

Dave Etter

FAILING

A failing bank in a failing town,
the president of the bank shot dead
for foreclosing on a failing farm,
the farmer, turned fugitive, not caught yet.

The slow hound sleeps away his last days
on the railroad ties of no trains.

A big old boy they call C.W.
says to me in the Harvest Moon Cafe,
"You done using that there ketchup?"

Folks sipping coffee in the back booth
talking on what used to be in town
but isn't any longer in town.

There's the bank president's daughter out there.
She strolls down the broken sidewalk,
cool and prim as a dining-car rose.
She married safe money in another town.

The jukebox snuffs out locals' local chatter.
The jukebox plays Eddy Arnold's
(ah, yes, yes) "Make the World Go Away."

C.W. puts plenty of Heinz ketchup
in his bowl of broccoli soup,
crumbles plenty of crackers on top.

"Don't tell me about no Reaganomics
and nothing about Reagan, neither."

The banker's casket is in the ground now.
Not too many friends came around.
The day is hot and dry, corn withers.
The weather has failed and failed again.

Stella Lynch: THE OPPOSITE SEX

You bet he was there last Saturday night,
him with all that bleached blond hair,
with his thunder and lightning shirt,
with his merry-go-round pants,
with his dude-ranch cowboy boots.
He was liquored up like a payday coal miner.
He made no effort to dance with any of us.
He was looking all over for you,
asking everybody where you was at.
"Say, where's May, where's May?" he says,
popping his gum, grinning like a fool.
If you ask me, he's a real creep.
I'd like to see him mess around after me.
I got an old man and two brothers
which are all about half crazy.
They'd pour gasoline on top of him
and melt that tail of his down to the ground.
It's guys like him what take all the fun
out of these country-western dances.
There's always at least one of his type,
always someone with a Texas-size mouth
and some refried beans for brains.
If I was you, I'd stay the hell away
from the Masonic Temple, the Dew Drop Inn,
from the Sunset Bowling Lanes,
from the corner of Sixth and Main,
and the roller rink too, if I could.
But, hey, pay no mind to me, May.
There's some of you peculiar folks
who just can't wait to take on trouble.

Walter Ingram: IN THE MIDDLE OF THE MIDDLE WEST

Often on hot, humid summer nights,
if I am bored or terribly lonely,
I like to rip up the backcountry roads,
pushing my big blue Buick until she bounces
past corncrib, windmill, and cow barn.
But I also like to just creep along
and look into a lighted farmhouse
where the family is reading the news,
watching television, or playing cards,
or where a boy in a Cubs baseball cap
is tacking a pennant to his bedroom wall,
or where, hopefully, a pretty girl
is walking the kitchen floor in her slip.
It is then I start to glow,
to feel affectionate toward people again.

But this evening I have had too much gin.
The katydids are shrilling in the darkness.
And I am fresh out of love.

The roads, the farms, the good folks
who live on those islands in the corn
will have to wait for that other me.

Damn, it is hard to stay sober here
when one day yawns into the next
and there is little nerve left
to scale the fence, fly the coop.

The Buick sulks under the sullen leaves.

I pass out in my overstuffed chair.

I am being buried half alive
among the tired smiles of used-car salesmen
in the middle of the Middle West.

LIVE AT THE SILVER DOLLAR

(*Another Late-Night Fantasy*)

Saturday night.
The place is packed to the door
with farmers, merchants, college kids,
and guys getting out of the cold.
The microphone works,
the introduction has been made,
and by golly I am, at last,
live at the Silver Dollar.
Radios all over the state of Minnesota
are turned on, turned up
so as not to miss my first poem.
a poem that will lead
to thirty minutes of poems,
all mine, all going out
live at the Silver Dollar.
Where now is the place?
Ghent, Minnesota, is where.
The Silver Dollar in Ghent, Minnesota,
the first Gopher State bar
to reopen after Prohibition.
I say, "Thank you very much"
to the applause
that follows each poem I read.
A Southwest State coed,
"Bambi" spelled out over her left breast,
moistens her upper lip
and closes her big brown eyes.
A carpet salesman
from Cottonwood County,
his hairy hand on a cold jukebox,
takes out an order blank
and jots down the title
of my new book.
Man, oh man, oh man,
what a perfect night,
what a crazy kick it is for me to be
live at the Silver Dollar!

TOWN NAMES

We have names of towns here in Illinois that would brighten up any man's gazetteer. Names that sparkle on the tongue. Names that dazzle the tourist's eye whenever he reads them on city limits sign, town water tank, or down at the depot. I mean town names such as Alsip, Arcola, and Ashkum. Names such as Blue Island, Buffalo Grove, and Bulpitt. Names such as Cahokia, Carbon Cliff, and Cobden. Names such as Illiopolis, Indianola, and Iuka. "Don't forget Equality," Doreen says, sticking a stub of Charleston Chew between her teeth. We also have a string of pretty fair M towns: Mahomet, Mascoutah, Mattoon, Mendota, Meredosia, Metamora, Metropolis (Superman's hometown) and Midlothian. "Don't leave out Karnak or Onarga or Peotone," Doreen says, her right cheek bulging now with a cherry lollipop. "Or Rantoul or Scales Mound," I tell her. Then, there are those terrific T towns: Table Grove, Tallula, Teutopolis, Thebes, Timewell, Tolono, Toluca, and Tower Hill. Doreen laughs. "What's so funny, sweet-tooth girl?" I say. She takes the candy out of her red-sticky mouth. "Remember that wedding announcement in one of the local papers?" she says. "I know, I know," I say. "It went like this: NORMAL MAN TO MARRY OBLONG WOMAN" —Normal and Oblong referring to two Illinois towns. "Boy, everyone sure had a good chuckle over that one." Doreen laughs again. "I wonder if they are still married?" she says. "I wouldn't be surprised," I say. "And they probably have about six kids by now, three normal and three oblong."

BASEBALL

We stand for "The Star-Spangled Banner." The home-plate umpire shouts "Play ball!" The leadoff batter spits tobacco juice through his teeth. The pitcher spits. The catcher spits. The first baseman spits into his glove and rubs it in with the heel of his hand. The second baseman spits on the infield dirt, and so does the rookie shortstop, who, being a bit nervous, just called up from the Iowa farm club, dribbles some spit on his chin. The third baseman spits. The pitcher spits again and checks the outfielders, who all spit at the same time. The first pitch of the game is a fastball strike, right over the outside corner of the plate. The batter turns his head, says a few angry words to the home-plate umpire, and spits. "Have an eye, ump," shouts the visiting team's manager from the dugout, and he spits a brown stream of Beech-Nut halfway to the third-base foul line.

David Allan Evans

THE MAN IN THE RENDERING ROOM

He works his eight-hour day inside
Armour's steam. The steam is his white
floor and his white ceiling. It keeps
belching up out of the six tank holes
after he jerks open their iron lids.
I rarely see him. Does the steam make
him shy, an animal in fog? I just get
glimpses of him.

But I can put him together. He is shirt-
less with a bulging chest. His back and
shoulders are the color of lobster. His
biceps, constantly working, are round and
seamed. When I get close enough I notice
he is always grinning. He never speaks.
He works by himself, without breaks. I
never see him puffing on a cigarette, lean-
ing against the handles of a tankage cart,
complaining about the pay or the heat.

The heat is too much for me. I can stay
no longer than it takes to dump my cart-
load of condemned heads or kidneys or bellies.

I take a deep breath before I go in. I roll
my cart in fast and look around for him. I
catch his finger pointing to the least-full
tank. By the time I get there the lid is
open and his pitchfork hands are ready. I
tip my cart over the hole as the steam belches
up under us, swirling and relentless, hammering
my face and forehead. He is on his knees;
he sticks his hands deep inside the cart,
up past his elbows, up to his red shoulders
and beyond, scooping, pulling, forking,
jerking everything out. His back and arms
and neck are matted with guts and worms.
I know he is grinning; his head keeps nod-
ding, as if he figures he can grab joy
out of anything I bring him.

NEXT MORNING

two swallows
flit and skim a drink

four geese
clamber up the bank into some weeds

you can hear a calf suck

what happened last night
or a thousand nights ago
doesn't matter

I thread a worm
and cast as far as I can

PIGS

I saw the fresh cow's
head the farmer flung into
the barn for the pigs
explode them into
the shadows and land
eyesup
between two feeders.

Minutes later, one pig,
then two, then two more
began to snuff their way
out of the shadows, toward
the head; two more,
one more, two more—
little round sharks testing
the odor of death...

soon the head was
at the center of a
whirlpool of feeding pigs,
then it was rising and
rolling all around—
wide eyes
coming up and going under—
not quite flying over
the barn floor but not
touching it either.

RETIRED FARMER

Maybe he dreamed of
new snow, of shiny handles.

This morning I saw
broom and yellow work-gloves
farm a glittering topsoil
off his porch,
heard on the sidewalk
a scraping, a *ping*
of grain flying
from a shovel.

Then he sat a half hour
in his gray '57 Ford
with the engine warming up,
as if, both hands on the wheel,
he figured he was in motion.

NEIGHBORS

They live alone
together,

she with her wide hind
and bird face,
he with his hung belly
and crewcut.

They never talk
but keep busy.

Today they are
washing windows
(each window together)
she on the inside,
he on the outside.
He squirts Windex
at her face,
she squirts Windex
at his face.

Now they are waving
to each other
with rags,

not smiling.

Linda Hasselstrom

HAYING: A FOUR-PART DEFINITION

I

When I was fourteen, my father bought a new John Deere 420
for me to drive. I'm thirty-four.
      Some summers I've missed:
away at other jobs, married, teaching.
      But I'm home for now.
For the twentieth spring he hitches up the mower,
mows the big yard, stops to sharpen sickles, straighten
sections, grease zerks.
      Impatient, he begins before he's ready,
plunges in. When he's made the first land
he stops the tractor, grins, says "I usually drive it in third"
(so do I, I growl for the twentieth year)
      pours himself some coffee.
I mow around the field in diminishing concentric squares
trying to write a poem about haying.

II

On the first round: alfalfa's purple smell.
On the third: redwing blackbirds fly up, screeching.
On the fourth: the cupped nest swings
from three plants; *on the fifth:* four chicks,
openmouthed, ride the nest down to die.
On the sixth: I remember the first time. They cheeped
while I carried the nest off the field. Two redwings
fluttered where it had stood. They never went near it;
a buzzard did. *On the tenth:* damp heat induces sleep.
On the twelfth: I watch the sickle slashing.
On the thirteenth: remember a story. A neighbor caught
his pants leg in the power takeoff. When his sons saw
the circling tractor he was a bloody lump, baseball-size.
On the fourteenth: calculate the temperature at
one hundred ten. The first hour ends.

On the twenty-eighth round: an eagle circles up the grove,
pursued by blackbirds. I think of the poem again:
seeking words for the heat, the pain between my shoulder blades,
the sweat bee stinging under my arm. For fierce hot time.
On the fortieth: I think of water. *On the forty-second:*
the sickle hits a fawn; his bleat pierces the tractor's chug
like cold water on a dusty throat. He lurches off.
There's no way to see them in the deep grass,
no way to miss. Still, we never tell my mother.
I begin to lose track, listening for loose bolts,
but around sixty my father finishes hitching up the rake,
waves me in for coffee. The second hour ends.

42

III

*hay 1. n. Grass or other plants such as clover or alfalfa,
cut and dried for fodder. Slang. A trifling amount of money.
Used only in negative phrases, especially in "that ain't hay."*

IV

Today I mowed ten acres of hay, laid
twenty tons of alfalfa down, raked
it into windrows for my father to stack
this afternoon. Tomorrow he'll gesture
to the two stacks and say, "Well,
we've started haying." In a month
the two of us will put up eighty tons;
by August perhaps one hundred ten.
Hay for the cattle against winter, pitched
out in the snow for their slow chewing, snow
blowing among the stems, drifting on their backs.

SCRUBBING PARSNIPS IN JANUARY

There's a modern sink just inside the door,
but I always scrub parsnips the old way:
with the hose, outside.
The sun shines, and it's forty degrees.

Icy water fans over my hands.
I scrub the clinging earth from white,
stalky roots, their legs splayed
like a man's.
           My mother washes them
outside to keep the dirt
out of the plumbing.

But there's another reason—
the strong earth smell,
the weak winter sun on my back,
chill wind and cold water, those white
limbs open, a thin trail of blood
where my topping knife slipped
and cut my finger.
           The rich blood threads
between two roots and blends with the clear
water, follows it down into the earth
for next year's crop.

HANDBOOK TO RANCHING

Don't spend any money.

To conserve energy,
when a pickup is not moving ahead
shut the motor off.
Starters and batteries are cheaper
than gasoline these days.
Waste not, want not.

Don't keep horses in the corrals.
If there's snow on the ground
a horse can get by in a pasture without water.

Get the calves fed and watered before noon.
John Lindsay used to say
if he didn't get the work done in the morning,
he might as well go fishing the rest of the day.

Don't take chances. Don't get caught in a storm.
A cow can take more weather than you can.

Don't scatter thistles or cheat grass;
stack them in one pile and burn it.

Scatter hay in little bunches so each cow
or yearling can have one to itself;
they won't eat hay
after they lay on it.

Don't waste feed; know how much
you're feeding to every animal.
A penny saved is a penny earned.
Never call a veterinarian if you can avoid it.

You can never tell what a bobtail cow will do.

INTERSTATE 90

For seventy torturous miles I have guided this rattling green
Honda along the Interstate, considering implications of the
various permutations of farms I have been passing, contemplating
history, and seeing no single other car, no vehicle of any kind.
I've been alone, perambulating in a westerly direction.

Then fast I meet a greenFord, two cattletrucksloaded,
a Kenworthhaulinglogs, a blackCorvette, a yellowCougar
and a furnituretruck, twocampers and a pickup pullingaboat,
huddled together, bumper-to-bumper.
            What are they afraid of?
The buffalo are gone or corralled; the Indians generally peaceable.
Then they're gone,
and I'm all alone in the rolling yellow prairie,
headed west toward Kadoka where I seem to remember
seeing a tree.

Overhead, two buzzards circle, circle,
turning their wrinkled necks so first one yellow eye,
then the other,
glares at me.
When they eat a dead calf,
they dip their hooked beaks first
into the soft brown eye.

Tom Hennen

GRAVEYARD

I can see right through these pine trees
Today in the rain.
They have gathered near the abandoned cemetery
On a prairie hill.
Because it's gloomy
They moan in one voice
Stand drooping in the mud.
Nothing can cheer them up.
Each one
Feels now
What it's like to be uprooted
Taken far from home
And planted in a rainy graveyard.
Each one goes into the coming night
As if entering a forest.
Each one points silently at the sky
Its sharp needles
The color
Of eternal life.

SOMEDAY, WHEN THE MACHINES ARE GONE

Silence will plant itself
Over the landscape like groves of oak
Dark, with no need to talk.
Generations of silence
Will live in one spot
Easily nourished
As earthworms.

IN THE SNOWY FOREST

Digging a grave
For the old bitch dog
The ground steams
With each breath.
Here the earth
Is sandy
Loose even in winter.
We all have many bodies
Softly buried.
Behind us
The years rub together
And sigh
Like pine tops.
Only the snow that falls
Doesn't know
The heaviness of bones.

LOVE FOR OTHER THINGS

It's easy to love a deer
But try to pick out insects and scrawny trees
To care about.
Love the puddle of lukewarm water
From last week's rain.
Leave the mountains alone for now.
Also the clear lakes surrounded by pines.
People are already lined up to admire them.
Get close to the things that slide away in the dark.
Think of the frost
That will crack our bones eventually.
Be grateful even for the boredom
That sometimes seems to involve the whole world,
Sometimes just the grass.

Jim Heynen

MY FATHER, STILL A FARMER

My father, still a farmer
at 62, wears overalls
like they used to. Stripes,
bronze buttons to light a match on,
bib pockets for nails
or scribbled notes with cattle prices.
Still comes from the outhouse
with the suspenders buttoned wrong,
prefers this accident to belts
which give him stomach aches
and don't let in the air from the side
where you need it
on those hot sultry days.

At night in slippers
and wool pants
he's only half the man.
It makes me want to know
about the overalls. Something
about the overalls.
It's when he's in
those overalls I've seen his old arms
spring like willow limbs
to take a sick sow by the ears
and set her up
or hay bales leaping shoulder high
as if they know he wants them there.

I know old cowboys ride good horses
and old hunters have good dogs,
but farmers never show their age
in such dependent ways. This is
a special secret, their way of getting on.
At night I'm left to wonder
at those limp and wrinkled stripes
hanging on the porch.
The strange and aged look,
implicit strength,
of old and idle men and things
waiting to become.

MORNING CHORES

In my bed I turned toward light
and the odor of work on my hands,
toward the moist clothes on the floor
with the barnyard still breathing in them.
Outside the chorus began:
roosters crowing, dogs barking,
but I was not sure of the dawn
until I heard myself calling the cows.
Dew collected on my shoes,
pigs rose from wet earth,
milk dripped from the udders of cows.
Everywhere the fresh urge of morning
led us into our story.
The cows ate from my hands,
the milk flowed from my hands.
What happened between, I didn't know
and didn't care. It was enough.

Today all I hear is that memory
as I rise in this suburban light,
knowing too well I am here:
my hands full of dishes, a bed
with two cats and a wife
whose love sinks with me in yearning
for the small voice we all leave bawling
in one lost field or another.

Still the residing light
for us who have lived among animals
is like a religion that stands
when the old church crumbles.
For to have moved with the beasts who know
more than reason or law
but who accept the sun in the morning
and the hands that feed them
is to have been the voice in a song
that no one is singing,
happier than one who praises
and knows he is praising.

Even now I can feel
as the city untangles around me
that constant flow in the earth
that wants to be glad.
I offer no more than I can
from a life that was fed among animals,
what follows me now in my going,
a dawn that never stops breaking.

OUR FARM/OUR FAMILY

Land there in Iowa lay so flat
we never dared run naked through the fields
and only joked of swimming nude
in the creek so close to the railroad.
Now and then we did pee in the clover
but only on dark nights when the neighbors
were inside with their four-cornered eyes.

All roads there were straight,
barns rode the horizon like ships,
the sun was hours in setting,
and on the heaviest summer nights
a laugh could be heard for a mile.
We learned to be cautious as that albino fox
the whole township hunted for years.

So we were never exposed
except to ourselves on Saturday nights
when, just after eight, our family of five
conspired in the dim-lit kitchen,
stark-naked around the galvanized tub.
We laughed and pinched and took turns
scrubbing and using the same water.

Sunday morning the wide church pews
were our final test. We passed: father,
brother, and I in our black suits and starched collars;
mother, tightened in her corset, black hat and veil;
sister, too fully developed, draped in her loose
brassiere and the dress that kept everything private.
We liked things this way: the inside, the out.

THE GREAT STRENGTH

Those who bulged from their shirts
like straw from tightly tied bales
who won fistfights at the fair,
caught the greased pig, wrestled a steer,
were strong men of the plains.
But the great strength was private,
known only to old farmers
who could see the power
hidden in the face of a peddler
or farmhand, in the strangely shaped body,
pinched shoulders and spreading hips,
bent over like hybrid grain in the wind.

When the fields had been cleared,
when the last hay was stacked,
the last fence fixed,
when the cellar was sealed for winter,
always, there was the accident,
and he would be there
with jackknife or pliers or bare hands,
his strength coming out
from all its secret parts.
For a moment we knew:
a wagon set upright,
a hand pulled free from moving gears.
It was all in the wrists, or the legs,
or the eyes. Afterwards

there was no excitement at all,
and only a few saw him fade back to his body.

COMING HOME TO SIOUX CENTER, IOWA, IN EARLY SPRING

The last snowbanks
litter the lawns
like dead sheep.
Cold air, brittle faces,
despair. Home
was never like this.

Still the farmers
keep their pact
with the earth,
in town tonight
with their black suits
and wintered hands
to pray for crops.

Through the glass
church doors, I see them:
reverent heads
in formal rows
bowing like frozen buds.
Under the dimmed lights
they pray.

Outside where I stand
there is no ray
of hope, no spring dove
singing against the night.
My feet grow cold
in the cold grass.

They come out singing
"Praise God from whom
all blessing flow...,"
gather in circles
around their white breath,
smile, and button-up.

If I were one of them now,
I'd go back to the dark farmhouse
and my happy wife.
We'd pray again
and then make love
in the old family bed,
a bed as cold and ready
as an empty grain bin.

Bill Holm

A CIRCLE OF PITCHFORKS

I

They used to call it a sheriff's sale.
Had one over by Scandia in the middle of the '30s.
My dad told me how
the sheriff would ride out to the farm
to auction off the farmer's goods for the bank.
All the neighbors would come with pitchforks
and gather in the yard—
"What am I bid for this cow?"
3 cents. 4 cents. No more bids.
If a stranger came in and bid a nickel
a circle of pitchforks gathered around him
and the bidding stopped.
Even in the grey light of memory
the windmill goes around uneasily.
The farmer's overalls
blow into the fork tines—
the striped overalls look like convict suits.
A smell of cowshit and wet hay seeps into everything.
The stranger wears tweed clothes
and a watch chain.
The sheriff's voice weakens
as he moves from hayrack to hayrack
holding up tools,
describing cattle and pigs
one at a time.

The space between those fork tines
is the air we all breathe.

II

"Resist much, obey little."
Walt Whitman told us.
To bring light!
That's the thing!
Somewhere in North Dakota
lignite gouged out of the prairies
is transformed into light.
But you are not in darkness, brothers,
for day to surprise you like a thief.
We are all sons of light,
sons of the day;
we are not of the night,
or of darkness.
Let us not sleep, as others do
but keep awake and be sober,

Those who sleep,
sleep at night,
and those who get drunk,
are drunk at night.

III

There is so much light in Minnesota.
The white faces brought here from Arctic Europe,
the lines of white birch in the white snow,
white ice like skin over the water,
even the pale sun seen through snow fog.
White churches, white steeples, white gravestones.

Come into an old cafe
in Ghent, or Fertile, or Holloway.
The air is steamy with cigarette smoke and frozen breath.
Collars up under a sea of hats pulled down,
you can hardly see the mouths moving under them.
The talk is low, not much laughing.
Eat some hot dish, some jello,
and have a little coffee and pie.
These are the men wrecking the ship of state—
The carriers of darkness.

Up in the cities
the freeway lights burn all night.

IV

My grandfather came out of Iceland
Where he took orders from the Danes and starved.
After he died, I found his homestead paper
signed by Teddy Roosevelt,
the red wax still clear and bright.
In the corner, a little drawing of a rising sun
and a farmer plowing his way toward it.
A quarter section, free and clear.
On his farm he found arrowheads
every time he turned the soil.
Free and clear. Out of Iceland.
In the thirties, the farm was eaten by a bank;
thrown back up when Olson
disobeyed the law that let them gorge.
In high school they teach
that Hubert Humphrey was a liberal
and Floyd Olson was a highway.

V

Out on the power line barricades
the old farmers are afraid their cows'
teats will dry up after giving strange milk,
and their corn will hum in the granary all night.

They have no science, no words, no law,
no eminent domain
over this prairie full of arrowheads and flowers,
only they know it
and the state does not.

We homestead in our bodies too,
a few years, and then go back
in a circle
faster than the speed of light.

SPRING WALK AROUND A SWEDE PRAIRIE SLOUGH

I

I saw this muskrat house before,
on a cliff a thousand feet
above the sea in Ireland;
a saint lived in it there,
not a muskrat; he prayed
alone and meditated.

II

Why the heap of fish bones
the smell of wet fur
a thousand years old?
Why does wind blow in Latin now
over the wattles at Conly's slough?

III

You never see anything right
till you see it twice;
once in this world, once
more in the other one.

THE ICELANDIC EMIGRATION TO MINNEOTA, MINNESOTA

I

After only a thousand years where they were,
In Vopnafjorthur, Floi and Jokulldal,
They left again, some for coffee, some for land,
Some no doubt for the hell of it, and came here.
They did not keep slaves, did not get capital,
Did not open any more wilderness. They farmed,
Grumbled, voted Republican, said their R's wrong,
Dreamed in genders. A few went out to the barn
With ropes, but from another few it dropped away
So quickly that after a few years you could
Not tell them from the others. By the next
Generation the names went wrong in the neigh-
bor's mouths; the R slipped off the teeth, and slid back
Into the throat. The dreams came in genders now
Only after whiskey, or when the last disease
Fastened its baling hook deep into the brain.

II

In the third generation, all that was left:
Sweet cake, small stories, a few words whose meaning
Slunk away to die under the mental stone
That buries all the lost languages of America.
The Mayans are there, Pequod and Penobscot,
And the Mandingo, and the Delaware Swedes.
The first tongue lost, did they acquire another?
The language of marketing and deterring
For the language of fish, poverty and poems?
In *The Invasion of the Body Snatchers*,
Seed pods open in your own closet at night,
Metastisizing into a body in-
distinguishable from your own, but the brain
Is something new, without memory, without
Passion, without you. Is this what it's like
To become a whole American at last?

OLD SOW ON THE ROAD

Thirty below. A hundred miles from home
the Buick throws a rod. Dead.
An hour later, I'm headed south
away from Paynesville in a truck.
A half mile out an old sow sits
on broken haunches in the middle
of the road. We stop. Maybe
fell off a stock truck; nobody
saw her in the iced-up mirror.
She swivels on that broken back, a pink
lazy Susan turning on the yellow line.
Ice blue light, gun barrel pavement
pink nose, snow, snow, more snow.
Airy colors for such a monster painting.
Windows iced tight, heater purrs loud,
but by God, I hear the howling
of that old sow, snout rotating, a double
barrelled gun aimed straight at me.
And that face! That face said everything
I'll ever say until I'm either dead
or alive as that sow at that moment
wanted so badly to be.

PIG

I have lain in the mud all day
Softening the bristles on my back,
Combing my ears on the box-elder tree
Till they stand up straight and pink.
Now I am going into the darkness—
To prepare for love.

Greg Keeler

DUCT TAPE PSALM

Take our broken lives
in thy bright grasp,
and make them to hold
fast until the bad weather.
Make our down jackets
to look like nuclear waste dumps.
Hold plastic table cloths
to the torn roofs of our
convertibles and seal
our cardboard windows.
Make our hoses and pipes to
spray sideways in many directions.
Hold our wrists tight
for the criminal while he
does his grim work.
Encircle our boots to
let water in and keep it there.
Mend our styrofoam coolers
when we glut them to cracking
with fish. Bond with Rubbermaid
to keep our trash
from the raging dogs,
and lash our dirtbikes
tight to the butts of our Winnebagos.
Hold slabs of contraband
to our bodies when we cross
national borders.
Make our Bibles, manuals and almanacs
to look like metalloid blocks
from Uranus. Never let us down.
Come loose when we least expect it.

ODE TO ROUGH FISH

I speak for the carp, fat on mud-bloat
and algae, orange-lipped lipper of algae surfaces,
round rotter of the banks of hydroelectric rivers.
Not the quick thin-meated trout
darting his pretty life in the rare rocks of high streams.

Ah, and the rooting sucker, round tubed mouth distended
to bobble rocks, worms, offal, whatever
he can turn up without himself turning up.

Yes, here's to you, scumsuckers of the stagnant
reservoirs and sludge-filled rivers, livers on
waste discharge, suckers down of anything we can
slop on you at our worst moments.

Long live you who will live long whether
we say so or not, who would as soon wallow in
the hollow of a bloated river-soaked moose corpse
as live up to a size 20 Coachman on a 7X tippet.
You live up to nothing and we will never live you down,
for you horrid-mouthed mouthers of death and
worse than death have found something stronger
than the slats of your hard flat scales.

Where a trout jumps for the thin wings of a fresh-
hatched caddis, you jump for nothing but air
through the filth and oil slicks.
Where a trout darts at a nymph behind a rock, you
could care less; you move the sonofabitching rock
and all the mud around it. Yes, you too will
find the nymph and eat it, but you will also eat
the mud and love it.
Yes, you love mud.
Mud is your guts; thus, your guts are always distended
in thick slabs of carp meat—sucker meat.
You and your wallowing, blubbery truth.
You and your truth that has made a heaven of sewage.

Why didn't they call YOU rainbow or golden,
for if God gave a promise and warning
in one fell swoop,
you are it,
arching from your black lake
completely clear and shining of water
then falling back
splat.

MAIL-ORDER SESTINA
(Ulysses, Kansas)

It figures that your mother was a mail-order
bride: Brooklyn Girl Marries Kansas Farmer—
that you and your new father didn't speak
for six years. "Tell her to pass
the mashed potatoes"—that the farm dusted over
bad and you sat in it for summers before it grew

back. But you accepted it, grew
used to the older step brothers and sister ordering
you around until you ran off and got over
it in the only tree for miles, watching some farmer
turn the late stubble to dust. It wouldn't pass.
This father wouldn't speak.

But one day he got the horse to speak,
dragging it to death behind the truck. You grew
as other animals died. Your rabbit, Pinky, passed
like this: the cat bit off its head. Order
restored that night, the stiff-jawed farmer
said, "Pass the rabbit," as the skies slid over

prop drones then webs of vapor trails, over
the dust that never settled, the catbird that spoke
all night. For years the short, burned sons of farmers
around you married daughters who knew their language, grew
their children young. For you the orders
stopped. You stuck by your mother as she passed

her arms through rooting pigs until the pain passed
from work that never fit. Years later, over
Kansas backroads, you returned and found order
in the rafters of your attic, chickens speaking
through carcasses of rabbits. This grew.
Once you returned to a chinchilla farm,

furballs scratching sand around your bed. Forms
darker than rusting sheds followed summers, passing
beyond where you drove the tractor, monotony grooving
the sun away in wind that didn't quit in over-
cast or gullies scorched to cracking. Speaking
his first words to you, that father ordered

more than you could take. So you left the farm,
hopped in a pink '57 Chevy and passed
from him and the world until you grew.

60

LONG LAKE, MINNESOTA

When I was four, Father rowed
me out to weed beds of sunfish
so big our bobbers dove
red and white to deep green. Foolish

bundle I was, I romped and screamed
'til he tied me to the seat,
afraid I'd drown us both. I dream
those days now, bright

bobbers moving through sleep,
pulled down by life I can't control,
but then I was life that deep,
and Mother stood above the roll

of perfect waves, waving in a green
coat beside my brother, stung red
by hornets. On water I've never seen,
I try to get back to Brother Ted,

to Mother, but Father is gone
and the boat drifts in and out
of fog and dreams slipping down the dawn
of a thousand lakes, scattered about

like lost coins in the woods
of Minnesota. Now, years later
I look down from a jet, tied
to my seat, and blur the sun to water.

Michael Kincaid

MEDICINE HOLE

Killdeer Mountain shimmers in the heat,
bending its horizons.
At its crest is the hole where the warriors disappeared.
Nighthawks sleep with open eyes on the bare stone.

The hole stands open like a chimney no longer used;
pebbles rattle down into the dark.
A hundred years ago,
surrounded men escaped by taking that way out.

I stare into the cleft whose dark gives birth to legends.
I smile to my friend—
those men are here.

Deep in midday dreams,
the nighthawk keeps his watch.

BADLANDS TALISMAN

This antler is a power sprung from the head
of mystery,
left here as a gift.
The battles of power are dreaming in its curves.

Bare desert branch whose birds have left it
to an elegant solitude,
the color of clay turning into sky.

Weapon the earth will now wear to all its wars.

Hefted in my hand,
a divining rod whose weight denotes the earth,
whose tips find heaven in all directions.

This lightning of bone electrifies my touch.
Hunting back along its curves,
I find the creature it belongs to.

William Kloefkorn

ALONE IN THE SANDHILLS OF SHERIDAN COUNTY, NEBRASKA STANDING NEAR THE GRAVE OF MARI SANDOZ

She holds to her silence
as if death can be in fact
conclusive,
the lark meanwhile
from atop its perch of soapweed
stirring the warm June air
with the wand of its
high sudden song.

And this hillside, this delicate hogback,
how the late afternoon sun
shimmers its coarse green skin,
switchgrass and snakegrass and grama,
and above it all the wide bellies
of the Hereford and the Angus,
their calves beside them
red and black in the sunlight,
shimmering. And nearby the orchard,
Old Jules' apple and peach and plum trees
in a long thick line of open defiance,
beyond them the lowland meadow
sweet with impending hay,
and standing here
alone in the Sandhills
of Sheridan County Nebraska,
near the grave of Mari Sandoz,
I would think something true
to match the perfect pitch of the lark,
against one of the barbs guarding the grave
would puncture myself to blood
to know and to keep it:
that I am alive
at this X my bootheel marks
in the earth of Sheridan County,
that above me the flash of the redwing
omens the blue sky now and tomorrow,
that I am as surely the object
of the kingbird's eye as I am
observer.

Until the gathering cirrus
begins to deplete the sun:
the throat of the pulley
when I push back the gravegate
whines. At my ankles
persist the burrs of lost uprisings,
lost intentions, lost loves,
while underfoot the grit
for all its eternal shifting
never moves.

CORNSILK
—*for Alva Foil Baker*

My wife's father is about to be buried.
The minister is saying something
rapidly becoming final.
Under the edge of the canopy,
canopy bluer far than any Kansas sky's blue,
I hold my grandson of almost sixteen months.
A steady southern breeze upblows his hair,
cornsilk of the very highest order

suspended, and I turn us slowly clockwise
because I am playing the game called
viewing the world through the upblown suspended
cornsilk hair of my grandson: O
cornsilk the Chinese elm and the wide green catalpa,
cornsilk the red earth fresh from plowing,
cornsilk the high August sun, the western horizon,
cornsilk the buffalo grass and the near nervous

cornsilk sweep of the kingbird,
and under the spray of red carnations
cornsilk the mind's last memory of my wife's father,
all the days of his life recounted
as if strands of cornsilk
moving light and eternal
in a warm fixed partial
hour of wind.

from *Houses and Beyond*
FROM WITHIN THE FIRST HOUSE

From within the first house
I looked out one early morning
to see the milkcow
looking back at me,
her eyes huge and clear,
a tuft of green dung
clinging to her udder.
She stood wide and solid,
the veins in her neck
explosive—
yet something in the chewing
of her cud suggested mystery.
So out of myself
I found myself uncurling:
into the window's glass,
into the dawn of air and eye
beyond the glass repairing.
And here is what the cow
was wondering:
why her milker
had left her standing there
unstripped
that pale, peculiar evening:
had dragged the bucket of milk,
aslosh and bottom-heavy,
across the lot
and over the yard
and up the steps
and out of everything
except for hearing.
And then the silence.
And then the night.
And then the early morning.

And then the screaming.

And then the hands forever
of someone else,
the forehead at the flank
less warm, less reassuring.
And I said to the cow:
I was born that morning.
I arrived trailing the seventh scream.
And the one who left you standing
is my mother.

She is asleep now,
and I am beside her,
at her breast, beholding.
And listen:
this is the first time in all my days
that I have seen things clearly.
And O how fresh, how sweet the world is!
It is a house of milk and tongue
and eye and skin
and breath and breast and quilt
and fingertips and dung,
and that is all it is.

And that is everything!

FROM *PLATTE VALLEY HOMESTEAD*

Wind in the break
sings low tonight
for the children,
sings cedar,
sings pine
for the children,
tamarack switch
not a switch tonight

but a string
being played
by the wind
in the break
for the children,
the roots of the trees
in the break
sounding-boards

for the children,
sing cedar,
sing pine
for the children,
for the bones
of the little children
in the hayfield
fallow and cold.

FROM *PLATTE VALLEY HOMESTEAD*

Punch a thumb into this Platte Valley soil,
and if the thumb is longer than a moment
you'll strike a mother lode
far richer even
than a good rainwater cistern.

Even so, Anna with a length of willow
witches for water: Voodoo Anna,
her wild hair stilled for the moment
beneath a scarf of red bandana,
the limb in her hands as if a plowbeam
hitched to the tough slow movement
of an invisible mare.

When the willow quivers and trembles,
and plunges downward,
Anna shouts *Hoka-hey*!
as if her own sweet skin,
and not the earth's beneath her,
had been broken.

The windmill rises straight and clean
and incredibly new,
its wheel impatient to catch the wind,
its shaft the latest onset
of perpetual motion.

The first of the water
gurgles out of the spout
and down the trough
and splashing against our hands
falls into the deep round silver metal tank.

Anna stands to shake her wet palms above me,
a little christening,
and I look up to see
a circle of sunspots
flashing their semaphore
to the remotest byway in the valley.
Whoever is thirsty, whatever is thirsty,
wherever you are, old man, old beast,
old woman, old bird,
if you are thirsty,
come, come to the well and drink.

FROM *PLATTE VALLEY HOMESTEAD*

Anna snaps the long full ears of sweetcorn
into shorter pan-sized pieces,
and from my chair at the kitchen table
I tell her she must be half Pawnee at least,
taking always with her, as she does,
the center of the universe.
Your white man's mouth, she says,
dropping the corn into boiling water,
is full of talk because your hands are empty:
up from your white man's throne, she says,
and mash the potatoes.

  Through steam rising
  from porkchop gravy
  I watch the boys
  like blue-eyed beaver
  gnaw the corn.
  No matter the size
  of the acreage,
  a quarter here,
  an acre there
  tacked on,
  it comes to this:
  supper in a bright
  warm kitchen,
  the river in a circle
  flowing,
  clear water
  over fine clean sand,
  small world
  but O good God above!
  Earth Mother here below!
  immense! Immense!

Amen.

Ted Kooser

A POETRY READING

Once you were young along a river, tree to tree,
with sleek black wings and red shoulders.
You sang for yourself but all of them listened to you.

Now you're an old blue heron with yellow eyes
and a gray neck tough as a snake.
You open your book on its spine, a split fish,
and pick over the difficult ribs,
turning your better eye down to the work
of eating your words as you go.

CENTRAL

As fine a piece of furniture
as any Steinway, all oak
and nickel and Bakelite,
her switchboard stood in the kitchen
stretching the truth. While she sat
with her ear to the valley,
rumor reached its red tendrils
from socket to socket, from farm
to farm. When the sun went down,
she sat in the dark. Those voices
she'd listened to all afternoon,
clear as the high sharp cries of geese,
flew over the house and were gone.
The loose lines buzzed. In the moonlight,
her hands held the wilted bouquets
of pink rubber. "Central," she'd say
to the darkness. "This is Central.
Hello? Is there anyone there?"

VISITING MOUNTAINS

The plains ignore us,
but these mountains listen,
an audience of thousands
holding its breath
in each rock. Climbing,
we pick our way
over the skulls of small talk.
On the prairies below us,
the grass leans this way and that
in discussion;
words fly away like corn shucks
over the fields.
Here, lost in a mountain's
attention, there's nothing to say.

PORCH SWING IN SEPTEMBER

The porch swing hangs fixed in a morning sun
that bleaches its gray slats, its flowered cushion
whose flowers have faded, like those of summer,
and a small brown spider has hung out her web
on a line between porch post and chain
so that no one may swing without breaking it.
She is saying it's time that the swinging were done with,
time that the creaking and pinging and popping
that sang through the ceiling were past,
time now for the soft vibrations of moths,
the wasp tapping each board for an entrance,
the cool dewdrops to brush from her work
every morning, one world at a time.

70

SPRING PLOWING

West of Omaha the freshly plowed fields
steam in the night like lakes.
The smell of the earth floods over the roads.
The field mice are moving their nests
to the higher ground of fence rows,
the old among them crying out to the owls
to take them all. The paths in the grass
are loud with the squeak of their carts.
They keep their lanterns covered.

ABANDONED FARMHOUSE

He was a big man, says the size of his shoes
on a pile of broken dishes by the house;
a tall man too, says the length of the bed
in an upstairs room; and a good, God-fearing man,
says the Bible with a broken back
on the floor below the window, dusty with sun;
but not a man for farming, say the fields
cluttered with boulders and the leaky barn.

A woman lived with him, says the bedroom wall
papered with lilacs and the kitchen shelves
covered with oilcloth, and they had a child,
says the sandbox made from a tractor tire.
Money was scarce, say the jars of plum preserves
and canned tomatoes sealed in the cellar hole.
And the winters cold, say the rags in the window frames.
It was lonely here, says the narrow country road.

Something went wrong, says the empty house
in the weed-choked yard. Stones in the fields
say he was not a farmer; the still-sealed jars
in the cellar say she left in a nervous haste.
And the child? Its toys are strewn in the yard
like branches after a storm—a rubber cow,
a rusty tractor with a broken plow,
a doll in overalls. Something went wrong, they say.

SO THIS IS NEBRASKA

The gravel road rides with a slow gallop
over the fields, the telephone lines
streaming behind, its billow of dust
full of the sparks of redwing blackbirds.

On either side, those dear old ladies,
the loosening barns, their little windows
dulled by cataracts of hay and cobwebs
hide broken tractors under their skirts.

So this is Nebraska. A Sunday
afternoon; July. Driving along
with your hand out squeezing the air,
a meadowlark waiting on every post.

Behind a shelterbelt of cedars,
top-deep in hollyhocks, pollen and bees,
a pickup kicks its fenders off
and settles back to read the clouds.

You feel like that; you feel like letting
your tires go flat, like letting the mice
build a nest in your muffler, like being
no more than a truck in the weeds,

clucking with chickens or sticky with honey
or holding a skinny old man in your lap
while he watches the road, waiting
for someone to wave to. You feel like

waving. You feel like stopping the car
and dancing around on the road. You wave
instead and leave your hand out gliding
larklike over the wheat, over the houses.

Thomas McGrath

THE TROUBLE WITH THE TIMES
for Naomi Replansky

In this town the shops are all the same:
Bread, bullets, the usual flowers
Are sold but no one—no one, no one
Has a shop for angels,
No one sells orchid bread, no one
A silver bullet to kill a king.

No one in this town has heard
Of fox-fire rosaries—instead
They have catechisms of filthy shirts,
And their god goes by on crutches
In the stench of exhaust fumes and dirty stories.

No one is opening—even on credit—
A shop for the replacement of lost years.
No one sells treasure maps. No one
Retails a poem at so much per love.

No. It is necessary
To go down to the river where the bums at evening
Assemble their histories like cancelled stamps.
There you may find, perhaps, the purple
Weather, for nothing; the blue
Apples, free, the reddest
Antelope, coming down to drink at the river,
Given away.

SOMETHING IS DYING HERE

In a hundred places in North Dakota
Tame locomotives are sleeping
Inside the barricades of bourgeois flowers:
Zinnias, petunias, johnny-jump-ups—
Their once wild fur warming the public squares.

Something is dying here.
            And perhaps I, too—
My brain already full of the cloudy lignite of eternity...

I invoke an image of my strength.
            Nothing will come.
Oh—a homing lion perhaps
            made entirely of tame bees;
Or the chalice of an old storage battery, loaded
With the rancid electricity of the nineteen thirties
Cloud harps iconographic blood
Rusting in the burnt church of my flesh...

But nothing goes forward:
The locomotive never strays out of the flower corral
The mustang is inventing barbwire the bulls
Have put rings in their noses...

The dead here
Will leave behind a ring of autobodies,
Weather-eaten bones of cars where the stand-off failed—

            Strangers: go tell among the Companions:
These dead weren't put down by Cheyennes or Red Chinese:
The poison of their own sweet country has brought them here.

THE BUFFALO COAT

I see him moving, in his legendary fleece,
Between the superhighway and an Algonquin stone axe;
Between the wild tribes, in their lost heat,
And the dark blizzard of my Grandfather's coat;
Cold with the outdoor cold caught in the curls,
Smelling of the world before the poll tax.

And between the new macadam and the Scalp Act
They got him by the short hair; had him clipped
Who once was wild—and all five senses wild—
Printing the wild with his hoof's inflated script
Before the times was money in the bank,
Before it was a crime to be so mild.

But history is a fact, and moves on feet
Sharper than his, toward wallows deeper than.
And the myth that covered all his moving parts,
Grandfather's time had turned into a coat;
And what kept warm then, in the true world's cold
Is old and cold in a world his death began.

WINTER ROADS

In the spring thaw
The winter roads over the cold fields
Disappear
In front of the last shed.

All summer they sleep
Hidden and forgot
Under the green sea of the wheat.

Now, in autumn,
They rise,
Suddenly
Out of the golden stubble.
They arch their backs in the sun
And move slow and crooked across the fields
Looking for winter.

PRAISES

The vegetables please us, all modes and virtues.
                                        The demure heart
Of the lettuce inside its circular court, baroque ear
Of quiet under its rustling house of lace, pleases
Us.

   And the bold strength of the celery, its green Hispanic
¡Shout! its exclamatory confetti.
                              And the analogue that is Onion:
Ptolemaic astronomy and tearful allegory, the Platonic circles
Of His inexhaustible soul!
                           O and the straightforwardness
In the labyrinth of Cabbage, the infallible recitude of Homegrown
                                                        Mushroom
Under its cone of silence like a papal hat—
                              All these
Please us.
             And the syllabus of the corn,
                              that wampum,
                                        its golden
Roads leading out of the wigwams of its silky and youthful smoke;
The nobility of the dill, cool in its silences and cathedrals;
Tomatoes five-alarm fires in their musky barrios, peas
Asleep in their cartridge clips,
                           beetsblood,
                                   colonies of the imperial
Cauliflower, and the buddha-like seeds of the pepper
Turning their prayerwheels in the green gloom of their caves.
All these we praise: they please us all ways: these smallest virtues.
All these earth-given:
                     and the heaven-hung fruit also. . .
                                             As instance
Banana which continually makes angelic ears out of sour
Purses, or the winy abacus of the holy grape on its cross
Of alcohol, or the peach with its fur like a young girl's—
All these we praise: the winter in the flesh of the apple, and the sun
Domesticated under the orange's rind.
                              We praise
By the skin of our teeth, Persimmon, and Pawpaw's constant
Affair with gravity, and the proletariat of the pomegranate
Inside its leathery city.
                     And let us praise all these
As they please us: skin, flesh, flower, and the flowering
Bones of their seeds: from which come orchards: bees: honey:
Flowers, love's language, love, heart's ease, poems, praise.

76

Don Olsen

LINES COMPOSED AFTER A DRAWING OF MYSELF, IN MY GARAGE, SECRETLY READING POETRY TO A 1973 BUICK

Being and thought
  never coincide,
  even by chance.
      —Antonio Machado

I do it because you can't read poetry to the newer cars.
The newer models never understand. They're too concerned
with computerized controls and circuit boards.
The young cars just don't listen like the cars of old.
The new cars think that time's a digital display
of numbers progressing in a line. They will never sense
the circular motion of time through space, that time is space.

The older cars are more like me, with creaking, twisted frames,
with dents and rust and all their crucial inner parts
corroded by misuse and age. The old cars know
the stress and pain of getting started in the cold,
and the headlights of my car are mirrors
of my glazed and tired eyes. They stare straight ahead,
unwavering and stoic. With fenders hunched,
my Buick is a poor man's Sphinx, and I pretend to be
the William Butler Yeats of the garage,
where no second coming is at hand and no rough beast
is waiting to be born, but only a litter of cats.

I know my Buick doesn't hear me read. I know that.
I read poems to my car because it pleases me.
Had I lived a hundred years ago, I would have stood
in this same place and recited to a horse,
and his skin would shudder at each bad line
the way yours shudders now. A thousand years ago,
I would have read to a rock, an inexpressive,
flat-faced rock, and it would have been the same.

For it is always the same: I return to myself.
Again and again, I reach into myself, and write to myself,
and read to myself, alone, for I am no more than a rock,
a horse, a car—and I, too, neither listen nor really understand.

But I *feel* what I mean, and this is the way I want it to be,
and whether I go fast or slow, or coast or stop,
I read, I write, I live and love and disappear
into the endless, recurring cycle of time and space.
My headlights beam down the old roads as I travel and search
for the fatal collision of being and thought,
the intersection of my Self.

AUCTION

After farming poetry for twenty-five years I am retiring and will auction off my poetry farm and all implements next Saturday. Drive five miles north on state highway, turn at sewage lagoon and go west until you reach the old dump site, then turn south on gravel road and go past the rendering plant and follow direction signs from there.

SATURDAY 2:00

Diesel translator
Prose poem combine
Antique iambic cultivator
Carton of hand-made cliche filters
750 bales of couplets
Stainless steel inward image dip-stick
12' x 24' brooding house
300 gallon aluminum free verse tank
14' hog and poet feeder with grantmonger trough
12 packages of objective correlatives
Acme Easy Effort Electronic Alliterator
Epic compressor
Genuine leather surrealism harness
12 gauge oxymoron, like new
Hand-forged image chisel
4 h.p. metaphor pump

Tractor with hydraulic rhyme lift
16' sonnet silo
50 gallon drum of critical solvent
4 barrels doggerel detergent
Cast iron allegory funnel
Imported philosophical throttle
Gas powered internal rhymer
Self-propelled versifier with manure bucket
Panegyric syringe
Heavy duty revisor, needs work
Used palindrome, live and evil
Roll of transparent logic
50 lb. hexameter sledge
Line cutter with carbide tip blade
Galvanized simile dipper
Pun pen

Other items too numerous to mention

Coffee will be served on the grounds

ALEX ANDRINE ESTATE

Joe Paddock

THE MEETING HALL

as mist gathers in hollows
and the owl-mystery floats
earthward   peopie
from this region   of lakes
hills   farmfields   meet
in the upstairs of an old
wooden building   risen
from root and dream
the grandparents   culture
carried in the bone   built
this hall   to dance
perform stories from the secret
heart   make some blush
witn delight   and strong drink
nipped from the neck of dark
opens a shade
of the erotic   bodies
healthy as the moonlit swamp outdoors
turning on the worn floor   laughter
rumbles in tne living cnest
of a heavy-bodied young man
brown bottle hanging
from his hand   whose eyes
can hold no more   than one
perspiring girl with a flower in her hair
the calm ageless
man who directed the play
almost alone   closes
his eyes in strange
painful ecstasy   knows
the making of their children   the mating
of these bodies with the music
and lakes
                  hills
                        fields

LEAF DANCE, LIFE DANCE

Oak leaves, walnut, willow and ash . . . .
I rake and haul, heave barrel after barrel
onto the fenced-in compost heap, till full
for the tenth time, and I toss my beagle over
the fence, climb the little ladder and leap after,
and we dance the pile down.

This is what we live for.
We stomp and leap and roll,
and Ring's sometimes almost altogether
gone, as he sounds after something which stinks
(dead sparrow or tire-smashed squirrel),
just the whipping white tip of his tail
which I sometimes grip till he flounders
to the surface, his eyes filled
with immense light. *"Down there!"*
Down there!" Every writhing nuance
of his body speaks: *"Down there!"*

So much life *must* love death,
its smell and promise. Up and down!
Up and down! We leap and roll and dance,
smashing dead
leaves down tighter and tighter in the pile.

And even now
a new dance begins which will flame
high in spring,
when I mix in manure and the sun
leans near, and insects, worms
and forty billion bacteria to some incredible power
swarm in this ton of leaves. Up and down!
Up and down! Leap and dance! Snarl and eat!
Die in again
for sheer joy!

SAUNA

A memory of women.

I was only three. We took a trip to the Upper Peninsula of Michigan. To the little subsistence farm my mother grew up on. In an area settled by Finnish immigrants. In the deep woods. The big unpainted sauna building caught and held my attention. Ancestral memory, maybe. The sauna was heated up, I'd guess, a couple times a week. Being so young, I was given a choice: did I want to sauna with the men or the women? Wise beyond my years, I chose the women.

What a scene that sauna. What a sprawl of naked woman flesh. On benches that rose ever higher into heat. Fair-skinned, green-eyed young women with big breasts. Wrinkled old women with hanging dugs and burning eyes. Who cackled and spit Finnish into the scorched air. Scooped up a dipper of water from a big pail. Threw it onto super-heated rocks atop the stove. It exploded in steam:

HISSSSSSSSSSSSSSSSSS!

Swat! Someone had spanked me with a bundle of oak leaves. Ow! Those women all had oak leaves in their hands. Were spanking each other. Till the skin of their bare bodies turned red. I was swatted again and again. Cried out at this undeserved licking. Grabbed at their leaves. Laughed when they laughed at me. Someone hugged me up in her flesh. Carried me to the top bench.

HISSSSSSSSSSSSSSSSSS!

Burning oak and maple and apple popped and crackled in the stove. The heat within those woman-arms was just too intense. I fought my way downward through laughter. Don't know if I knew yet how to swear, but, *goddamn!* what had life in store for the likes of me? And SLOSH! a pail of cold water was dumped over my humming head. I screamed and beat, with small hard fists, the naked back of my mother. *Goddamn!*

The wet and shining naked bodies of those women have lived in me down through the decades. That image a humming hive in this mind. Bristling with stings. Pouring honey.

Nancy Paddock

PILOT KNOB

High above their scattered farms
and wooded gullies
the first settlers climbed
long hills with shovels
to leave their dead on Pilot Knob.

Now this graveyard is abandoned to the quick
deer which haunt these hills
and lovers who die
into each other in the dark.

Some stones are buried
in budding lilacs gone wild.
Iron fences, bent and tangled with branches,
keep out nothing that grows.

Some stones are sinking under grass,
broken puzzles, solved
only by the rain,
washing them clean
of human names.

The farmer who owns this hill
plowed up a marker last fall,
erased the two-track road.
This, too large a spot to leave to history.
He is making his own monument
of fieldstones here.

Even the dead have abandoned this place.
The few anyone remembered were dug out long ago
and their graves fall into themselves
like empty nests unraveling.

The rest are not held
in memory, but released
into the flow of things.
Most of them so young that death is a game—
they play hide and seek,
slipping into roots.

We can find them
in the incense of opening lilacs
and the resurrection of the April grass.

GOING OUT TO GET THE MAIL

across this whole prairie
nothing
to stop the wind
that bends
everything that will bend
and dries and shakes
human structures to dust

in shifting patterns snow
snakes across the road
sweeping plowed fields clean
filling ditches
the wind
an army
driving everything before it

highway signs shudder at their posts

nothing stays the same
the horizon has gone
white
leaving me exposed
as a lightning rod

nothing to stop the sky's
bare-taloned drop
to cover me with white wings

coming back
swimming hard
almost drowning in this current
breath is a dry gasp
a burning in the nostrils

thick crows yell from the bare grove
and the snow
has nearly covered my tracks
over the broken field

THE SILOS

All week she watched
the silo grow from concrete staves.
He had to have it,
this seventh silo—
(each one larger than the last).
And now they line one side of the drive,
half-circling the old house
with a great question
she dares not ask.

That house
with its drafty kitchen and slant floors—
nothing but a shelter for the night
when no work can be done.
(Real time spent with machines.)
He said, when they were married,
eighteen years ago this spring,
he'd tear its boards to shedwood and kindling,
build her a real home
on the wooded knoll.

But now that hill is planted
straight in corn
rows up one side and down
and as the sky fades,
fragile as a broken
, robin's egg,
silos loom around her
like black corridors
a woman could get lost in.

MAKING BREAD

Wheat berries ground in my handmill,
oil of seeds that have followed
the summer sun,
honey, each spoonful the life
work of a bee.

All these lives blend
with sea salt and yeast
in my grandmother's bread bowl.
I stir with her spoon
that is worn
flat on one side from years
she made bread

And then the dough, brown
as a summer child,
rolls over and over,
elastic young flesh in my hands.
Yeast creatures lift it round
as the belly
of the earth.

I form loaves that are nets
to catch the sun.
And when the winter kitchen
warms,
rich with its smell,
we eat
and an ancient strength
flows into us
out of the ground.

David Pichaske

FARM REPORT, WESTERN MINNESOTA 10/26/85

Ollie Johnson was talking bumper crop last night at the Silver Dollar Bar,
and for all I know he's right. Still,
his International Harvester 1480 left one hell of a lot of corn behind
when it rolled through these fields this morning.
Assured that he's taken what he wants, I sling an old mail bag
around my neck and track rows of stubble, gleaning winter food
for squirrels, rabbits, pheasant and deer.
                                    The work is child's play.
Dull golden against the black earth, whole ears of corn flash up at me,
picked and shucked, fallen between the combine's steel teeth...
or half ears, sliced vertically or horizontally, lost in the cracks
of a modern, mechanized harvest.
                          End rows especially
have given Ollie a rough time: he's flattened stalks
without so much as scratching the grain. These ears are most fun: a kick
of green boot confirms my eye's suspicion. I bend down, grasp
the ear with my left hand, the stalk with my right.
One quick snap frees ear from stalk. I slide
the yellow corn easily from its brown husk and pop it
in my mail bag. Ten minutes fills the bag. Like a field hand
dragging his sack of cotton, I trundle my mail bag to the ditch, empty it into
a cardboard box, and return to the rows of stubble.
                                    Ten minutes more, and
another bag, and yet another. Corn is everywhere, it seems: the more I glean
the more I discover: three, four, five feet of a row untouched,
just lying there waiting for me to bend over and pick it up.
This game I have met before in dreams: the coins—nickels and pennies at first
on the floor beneath the bed or beside the road. I lean down to
gather them in, and see dimes and quarters, even a bill or two.
Money, free for the taking...and always, the more I gather,
the more I find.
                Fantasizing,
I multiply $2.50 a bushel times perhaps five bushels an hour, might make
a good wage and an honorable living one month of the year,
and maybe help Ollie with his volunteer corn problem. Then I think
not of pheasant and deer, but of the world's hungry:
how many children will die today who might be walking these dreary acres
of western Minnesota, picking up the golden ears or the bushels of soybeans
that will elude Ollie's 1480? Not to mention, of course,
the scrawny beans on the south 40, too thin to bother harvesting?
We could get this thing going, I think: a gleaning for World Hunger.
Kids from the high school could do it, or even the poor themselves,
flown in from everywhere to glean the golden leftovers
of American agriculture, Texas to Canada, Ohio to Montana.

86

        I see us here
in Minneota, together, singing perhaps, and gathering great bags of beans
        and corn,
soyburgers and tortillas warming for lunch and dinner. And always,
the more we gather, the more appears. An American vision.
                                        Broken, even
as I dream it, by Ollie Johnson himself, nearly on top of me in his John
        Deere 8850,
trailing a disc, bearing down upon us all full bore. Ollie,
it's me, your tenant. These are the Minneota school children, the world's
        hungry,
for whom you will pray tomorrow in church.
                        We all shout together, but
Ollie is listening in his cab to the Minnesota-Ohio State football game, and
his mind is set on the 160 up by Taunton. He discs right through us,
slicing most of the remaining corn to a hash. I dive out of the way just in time,
and when I pick myself up, the Minneota school kids and the world's hungry
are nowhere to be seen.
                        Reclaiming my mail bag, I survey
what's left, think maybe the deer can make do with those butt ends of corn
that have not been turned under. And I set to work again,
more slowly now, reclaiming fragments of a dream.
                                        But it's Ollie's son
this time, with a plow. The underdog Gophers are upsetting the Buckeyes, and
if the weather holds he can get this whole section plowed before tonight's
        dance.
The corn is in, his father has told him, and prices piss poor this year. Time
to get on with next year's crop and make a better job of it then.
The black earth shines in his wake, ready for seeding into corn or beans come
        spring
or, should winter delay, into wheat this fall.
                        What more can I say? The harvest
is in, the fields are fall plowed. We're ready. And that, America,
is the farm report this middle October from Western Minnesota.

VISITING THE FATHER

You will find him in the basement,
behind the closed door of the old coal bin,
now his workroom. He is still there,
splitting the shake shingles for your doll house,
putting another coat of paint on your box hockey game.
Sometimes he busies himself refinishing old furniture or,
as his wife puts it, "just puttering."
None of his work here involves money,
so you know it is important.

If you knock and give the secret password,
he will turn down the Cubs game on the radio,
wipe the sawdust from his hands, and open the door.
You can sit on the orange and yellow stool
and tell him once again how you caught the three-pound bass,
how your ballet teachers says you are nearly ready to go up on point
(or he will sit on the orange and yellow stool,
watch you jazz dance to "Baby, You're a Rich Man,"
help you saw and glue your wooden race car).

If you ask, he will tell you
important secrets that he has told no one ever before:
stories of his life before he met your mother,
what your name might have been if you hadn't been you,
how to throw a curve ball and how to draw a tree,
the proper time for planting radishes and tomatoes,
where the walleye hide in the winter.
If you ask, he will explain the thing he is making.
Yes, you can watch. Yes, you can help.

THE GRANDFATHERS

St. Paul's Cemetery after reading GIANTS IN THE EARTH

Gudmundson, Olson, Peturson, Josephson,
Williamson, Anderson, Olafson, Hallgrimson.

In these graves sleep the founders of the kingdom,
below the arching elms, their branches bowed
like the vaults of Trondheim Cathedral.

Hanson, Benson, Sigurdson, Peterson,
Björnson, Rafnson, Jonason, Henrickson.

In the cycles of seasons their lives unwound,
in fields of ripening corn and wheat,
in the white wilderness of prairie winter.

Nicholson, Erickson, Högnason, Johnson,
Thordarson, Thorsteinson, Magnuson, Guttormson.

Far beyond the western rim of Iowa
the sun sets over the grave of Johann Kristjan Johannson.
He dreams dreams unbroken as the snow-covered prairie.

TEACH YOUR CHILDREN WELL

"and feed them on your dreams"
—Crosby, Stills, Nash & Young

can tell you only what I have come to know:
clean, black cut of new-paved road
(always north and always uphill);
to either side, beans and corn awaiting the combine;
behind, hollow moon dragging her sullen face
toward dark tangle of the sluggish Spoon River
(cottonwood, deer, fox and pheasant);
ahead, flame of northern lights, aurora borealis,
and, always, firm distance of the pole star.

John Rezmerski

SOME GOOD THINGS LEFT AFTER THE WAR WITH THE SIOUX

My eyes welcome high grass,
green going yellow
shooting up
from old old earth
fed with hard-earned blood
and bled sweat.
This soil now marked by tractor tires
fed Amos Huggins in 1862
and feeds me now,
feeds you,
and the blood it has swallowed
never spoils the corn.
It is the magic of that blood,
red cells and white cells,
and clear yellow fluid
falling on the warm black earth,
that keeps legs pumping
up the valley and over the bluffs
to mourn the innocent,
to cherish the giving,
to pray with fast breath
to the breath of the land,
nitrogen rising
from remains of quiet and boastful alike,
seeping into the roots of rosebushes,
the strength of wheat,
the warmth of beans,
the sweetness of corn and pork,
the plumpness of lovers,
into children of grass and grain
and the spirit of the blood,
hundredproof blood,
drunk-making blood,
man-making blood,
blood contaminated only by blood,
into the children of the eye,
of the spleen,
of the brain and the voice,
into the welcomers of grass,
welcomers of dawn
on the blue and brown earth,
welcomers of silence
and forgivers of fire and the plow and old murders.

COUNTRY MUSIC

You know me, I am your neighbor,
the wayfaring stranger,
floating across the land
as free as anxiety.
I left home just to have
someplace to come back to.
Me and the highway are going on together
through the State of Sorry Affairs—
too many days, especially at night
behind the wheel,
following the wind
singing absentmindedly through
town after town. Eventually
everyone we meet looks familiar—
people in little towns like home,
nearly kind to strangers,
married forever one day at a time.
Their windows are clean enough
to see across the street.

As a kid in a town like this,
I was bored enough
to memorize the numbers on boxcars
lurching over the trestle across the river
and gone for good without me along.
The road that goes back home is lonelier
than the road that goes away.

I don't even know where this road goes,
except right on through wherever I am,
past the morning paper bundles
dumped onto sidewalks,
past the noise of factories downtown,
past the drunks falling against their car doors,
past the bedrooms of people
waiting for the other shoe to drop.
I put a quarter in an off-duty parking meter,
feeling like the town is a jukebox:

I remember a song to sing back to the wind:

> *I stole almost every thing I own,*
> *I got a cast-iron stomach*
> *and a heart of stone.*
> *Don't need nobody,*
> *just go it alone*
> *like a real old wild west hero.*

But you keep walking through my dreams
and I'm nearly ready
to love somebody now.

MIRACLE

A man who had gone through
a silage chopper almost up to his shoulder
told me he had not enjoyed it
exactly,
but he did remember being happy
at coming so close to salvation.
It was Sunday
and he had been repentant.
He had not seen God
exactly,
but he had heard him,
and he picked up just one eternal verity
before his damn fool uncle
switched off the machine.
The sound of the shredding arm, he said,
was shaped by God, and
came in clear syllables,
saying,
take it easy, damn you, take your time.

FAMILY MUSIC

Dad bought Mom a battered old upright
from neighbors who'd neglected for two generations
to notice it was out of tune.
They thought their kids just had no talent.
Mom had it tuned, so I began
three years of Saturday mornings
with Sister Mary Constantine.
In the convent music room half frozen
next to her grim habit,
I tried to turn dots and lines
into easy sounds of sailboats or flowers.
Her joy was the counterpoint
of my knuckles quick and red under
her baton rapping
the right time on my fingers on the wrong keys.

      "You didn't practice—it
      goes like this."

She'd elbow me to the end of the bench
and retrieve the flower music from the spinet
perfect as a funeral wreath.
I'd surrender my mother's five dollars and
run home to beg
to be allowed to quit.

      "Someday, you'll be
      glad I made you learn. Imagine
      how you'll feel when
      you go to a party and they
      want you to play something."

Mom would wish again she'd gone beyond
her mere eight years of lessons.

Once a month or so
I'd come home to find her occupied
with Mendelssohn or Stephen Foster.
She'd get up red when I came in.
She never thought she was good
enough for anyone to listen.

When we moved to a new house,
the scarred piano stayed behind.

Some nights I'd lie on my bedroom floor,
ear against the radio,
jealous of a Steinway or a faraway orchestra

cutting through the static with
Beethoven or Tschaikovsky. Once my father
looked in and laughed and
closed the door.

>"How come you're listening
>to that
>longhair stuff?"

He used to croon
cowboy songs while he shoveled coal.
In the tub, he'd holler Stephen Foster.
Dad did all the singing in our house, but
Mom played piano when we had one.
I never got past the second lesson book
but I learned how to listen to
somebody else's music.

WILLMAR AT NIGHT

I have been to Willmar, Minn.,
where the houses look pious.
At night they hear noises,
metal wheels squeaking and hissing,
the throb of engines biding their time.
The houses turn over in their sleep,
dreaming of following boxcars,
windows wide open, wind whupping
through parlors and bedrooms,
finally, in Fargo or St. Paul,
letting strangers enter
with whiskey and loud phonographs.
I have been to Willmar, slept in Willmar,
crossed the tracks in Willmar at night.

Barton Sutter

WHAT THE COUNTRY MAN KNOWS BY HEART

I

Why he lives there he can't say.
Silence is the rule.

But he knows where to look
When his wife is lost. He knows
Where the fish that get away go
And how to bring them back.
He's learned about lures
And knows how deep the bottom is.

He has been lost and found.
Where he lives moss grows everywhere.
He's made his way home
The way gulls fly through fog,
Find where water turns to stone.

In country covered with trees
He can find the heartwood
That burns best.
He can find his wife in smoke.

He knows where to look for rain
And why the wives of city men
Cannot stop dreaming of water.

II

When loons laugh, he waits
For what follows, feeling
The meaning of animal speech
Crawl in the base of his brain.

But he knows there are no words
To answer the question the owl has kept
Asking all these years.

He knows a man alone
Will begin to talk to himself
And why at last he begins to answer.

III

He would never say any of this.
He knows how often silence speaks
Better than words. He knows
Not to try to say as much.

But then he won't say either
How often he longs to break the rule,
How unspoken words writhe in his throat
And blood beats the walls of his heart.

NIGHT OUT

Ten p.m. Half lit, Lenny Benson
Roars up the highway,
Six-pack on the seat beside him.
He pounds the steering wheel, old friend,
The night has just begun.

Deer, driven out by haunch-high snow,
Crowd close to the road. Their eyes
Reflect headlights as well as anything
Put out by the highway men.

He stops at the Dew Drop Inn
For a quick one, picks up Diana.
The road is a frozen river.
Lenny fishtails all the way
To Thunder Bay and back.

Four a.m. The Dew Drop Inn's gone dark.
In the booth where she dropped, Diana
Dreams of another man.
And Lenny Benson, two parts drunk,
One part dream, one part Lenny Benson,
Slips in his chair, slips toward sleep, but fights it,
Aiming his empty beer glass like a flashlight
At the head of the dead wolf on the wall.

GENEVA

She was famous for kindness, Geneva.
And yet she could run down a hen
And chop off its head just like that.
"Macaroni!" I said, when I saw the insides,
And she crowed like a satisfied rooster.
I once watched her husband, the only man
I knew who had a mustache, string up
And slaughter a cow. I ran to Geneva
And buried my face in her lap. "Geneva,"
I said, "does it hurt?" "That old cow?"
Said Geneva. "Don't worry," she said.
"You don't feel a thing when you're dead."

Geneva giggled and taught me to piss
In the dark in a thunder jug.
I was from town and embarrassed,
But Geneva enjoyed that noise.
She taught me itchweed and outhouse.
She spanked me and wiped my ass.
She was a good one, Geneva.
The world was a joke, and everyone said:
"She's a real card, that Geneva."

She had warts and a nose, Geneva,
And a twisted smile with teeth,
But she also had beautiful daughters.
Hay and fresh faces and breasts.
They could cook. The kitchen had pails,
And everyone drank from the dipper.
I can taste the tang of the tin
And smell that slop-bucket stink
And the fragrance of bread on the table.
She was always baking, Geneva.

She taught me the stars, Geneva.
It was night. In the garden.
She was giving us something again:
Carrots, cucumbers, tomatoes, and such,
Everything cool and slick. "Chicken shit,"
Said Geneva. "That's the secret," she said.
My pants were all wet with the dew.
"Look at that," said Geneva
And showed me the star-spangled sky.
"It's a coloring book," said Geneva.
"It's all dot-to-dot. Don't you see?"

And I saw: The Sisters, The Hunter,
The Bull and The Bear, The Dipper
From which we all drank.

So I thank the stars for Geneva,
All of her muscles and fat, that
Quick chicken-killer, that ugly
She of the beautiful daughters
And prize-winning hogs, that woman
Of pickles and jam. Geneva,
She taught me the mud and the stars,
And when I am ready to die
She will come with her hatchet in hand
And her face like a kerosene lamp
And her dress all feathers and blood.

PINE CREEK PARISH HALL

If what we remember is what we are,
Then I'm the Pine Creek Parish Hall.
Who was that guy who played guitar
And testified there when I was small?

Wasn't it Gust? Gust Nordvall.
I believed everything. Jesus.
Today I doubt that I could recall
The creed if I tried. The place is

All that remains of my old-time religion:
Nameless faces, folding chairs,
A poorly converted pioneer cabin.
My dreams will often take me there,

And just as I enter, the music starts.
Those farmers who sneered at factory wages
Bellow the hymns they know by heart:
"The Old Rugged Cross" and "Rock of Ages."

Thom Tammaro

CLOSING THE CABIN

I

In the yawn of dusk,
We drift home in Minnesota autumn,
Reciting the litany once more:
Dock in; boathouse latched;
Rugs rolled; plugs pulled
Windows hinged; floors swept:
Pilots out; pipes drained;
Faucets opened, doors locked;
Hummingbird feeder taken down;
Key hanging in its secret place.

II

In the flicker of lights near the city's edge
We talk easily, gather within
All that the summer has given:
A great fish, slender and shiny,
Diving for bottom; loons calling
In the still afternoon;
Stars swirling above the rooftops.
Near home, vees of geese circle,
Circle in the shadows above us.

III

Later that night, we pause
On the stairs—winterward—
Unlock that other season
Where little puffs of winter dust
Rise when we open the door.

VIOLETS ON LON HALVERSON'S GRAVE

"I came to this spring field to pick violets.
But I loved this field so much I've slept here all night."
            —Yamabe No Akihito
               8th Century Japan

I

No one has visited you for years.
But this evening I found you at the
Far edge of the cemetery north of town,
Your headstone long toppled and cracked.
The carved letters smooth and gray to touch,
Telling me all I know of you:
"Born August 1, 1860, Norway.
Died August 1, 1892." And everything
Around you smothered in violets.

II

You did not come here to pick violets,
Nor to sleep here only for the night
Because you loved this field.
I imagine one rainy August afternoon
A few friends from your same Norwegian
Village gathered here along with the
Dutiful minister, solemn and grim, who
Dusted his hands after the gray prayer
Then walked toward town,
The prairie wide as the pastures of heaven.

III

Once in a book on wild flowers,
I read that Japanese women wove
Braids of violets to wear in their hair
To show constant love and humility
To their lovers.
And that pioneer women crushed
The velvety petals in bowls of rainwater
Gathered during prairie storms
And sipped the sweet water
To ease the pain of headaches,
Then tied bunches of fresh violets
With horse hair and placed them
In trunks, under pillows, and on
Window sills as blessings
For all around.

IV

And now I would add how under moon and stars
They grow without love, or thought, or kindness.
And how each life lived is its own orbit,
Spinning and gathering into garlands and blessings.
And that ten thousand petals and the
Shadows of ten thousand petals are unfolding
In a cemetery north of town, in the night,
As quiet and holy as the breath of God,
Fragrant and deep purple to yellow,
Spreading like pure light.

THE LOST LUNCH
*"One item that popped up during a vault cleaning [at the courthouse]
was a thirty to fifty year old lunch, officials said. The disintegrating
brown paper bag contained two very hard-boiled eggs and a shriveled
banana."*

(*AP*) Little Falls, MN.

Mother was ill that morning; later, Doc determined
It was the onset of the pneumonia that later took her
So I packed my own lunch: three oatmeal cookies,
Two hard-boiled eggs, and a banana, skipping
Mother's bratwurst on hard rolls and her usual
Hunk of blueberry pie wrapped in waxed paper.

Later that morning at coffee break, I sat
With Molly Jesperson, and we shared the oatmeal cookies,
She nibbled on one, and I ate two. It was then I worked
Up the nerve to invite her for lunch.

We decided on the blue plate special down at the
Little Falls Crystal Cafe: meatloaf, mashed potatoes
With giblet gravy, corn, rhubarb pie, and coffee.
We were even a little late getting back to the
Courthouse, but Molly said she didn't mind.

Tom, the janitor, stopped by later to say he put
My lunch sack in a box with some files and leather-
Bound volumes and set it on top the vault in the backroom
So he could move the desks and tables to sweep
The floor at noon. I meant to get it before I left

For the day and have it for supper, but for the
Rest of the day I gladly filed my share of
Property deeds, summonses, and marriage licenses,
Dreaming of Molly and me down at
The Little Falls Crystal Cafe.

But things didn't work out so.
Two weeks later mother got worse.
Doc thought she'd get the care she needed
At the Eventide Lutheran Home. She had a sunny room
There, and I visited her every lunch hour.
But she didn't make it through the summer.

And Molly? The Monday after our blue plate special
She didn't show for work. A friend of hers said she
Moved with her family to Minneapolis. Later that month
I saw her picture in the society pages of the *Tribune*.
She was engaged to a paper salesman from Duluth and
Planned a June wedding.

Nowadays, when I pass the Crystal Cafe
And see couples eating or sipping coffee,
I just get this pang in my stomach,
Not quite of hunger, but for that one shiny moment,
For that one bright lunch I had then lost.

RELIGIOUS EXPERIENCE IN CENTRAL MINNESOTA

*"A survey of 14 congregations, including Covenant, Lutheran,
Presbyterian, Roman Catholic, and independent congregations, show
how widespread are extraordinary religious experiences. . . ."*

(*AP*) St. Cloud, MN.

You probably thought these things went out with the last
Great Awakening when conversion in wholesale lots
Was the theme of the day and New Englanders cried out:
"O, I am going to Hell!" in moments of great
Religious fervor. At least most intellectuals think so.
But Lord, let me tell you what they've been finding
Here in central Minnesota.

The team from the University says 30% report
Unusual religious experiences—that's almost one-in-three.
And every demonination is susceptible, though Lutherans
Report the least number of extraordinary experiences.
You probably thought these kinds of things only
Happened to Baptists in places like Georgia,
Mississippi, and rural Iowa. Well, let me tell you.

You'd be astounded at what's going on here
In the region: voices, visions, people claiming
They've been communicated with through dreams.
It's enough to make you stop and think.
Who knows what it all means? The team
From the University will find out, I suspect.
They think their approach will revolutionize
Biblical studies since most research assumes
There are no angels running in plays for God.
From the stories they're telling, though,
Seems as though the Lord is calling
The whole game from the sidelines.

What's it all mean? I'll tell you
I don't know for sure, but they're taking
A survey and eventually someone from the
University will quantify all that data for us,
Tell us what it means. They're planning to print
It all up in a booklet: "Protection, Deception,
And Direction: Extraordinary Religious Experiences
In Central Minnesota." Then we can read all about
ERE (pronounced like the name of the Great Lake).

You'll read about the rural Foley women who
Claims her backyard elm tree sings in an angel's
Voice every Easter morning—neighbors think they've
Heard it, too. And then there's the Benton County
Family who regularly receives messages from a long-dead
Uncle, drowned in Little Rock Lake, always telling them
How good the fishing is on the other side.
Lots of heavenly voices and angelic visitations.
Three of ten Christians, mind you.
Always visions with lots of bright light.
Lots of extraordinary experiences.

The booklet will cost you next to nothing.
Anyone interested in pre-ordering today?
Should be an extraordinary book—
Save for the chapter on the Lutherans.
I don't know. It's all pretty strange to me.
Extraordinary. A mystery, you might say.

Mark Vinz

MIDCONTINENT

Something holds us here—
call it the madness of phone lines,
the pride of blizzards,
the love of wheels and wind.

Something holds us here,
where roads don't ever seem to end.
Our maps are letters home
we don't know where to send.

IN A DROUGHT YEAR
—for Joe Richardson

The barn was empty,
falling down,
the windmill bent
like a discarded paper hat.
We passed a hundred like it—
talked of mountains, surf,
anything to keep us from
the heat and dying corn—
until we stopped
to watch an orange moon rise
and string our breaths
across those cooling fields—
going nowhere,
but going home.

LOST AND FOUND

In the small cafe just off the interstate
they've taken down the photo of the local boy
who pitched in the big leagues for awhile.
Tired farmers visit back and forth
among the table tops and wives—
their round wives with flat accents,
high hair and deep laughs.
The special today is country roasted ham
with corn and bread and American fries.
What was his name, anyway—
the kid from here who used to be a star?
We'll never see another one like that.

HOMESTEADERS

I

When they came
some of them already knew
that here was more than flatness;
here at last was a place
where all things would be possible.

II

Call it ocean, call it desert;
trails move off in all directions—
tall grass, wheatfield, open range.
Everyone here is traveler.
No one knows the way.

III

The buffalo wallow is thick with prairie aster,
cornflower, gentian, blazing star.
We walk the fields till dusk,
when deer come down to drink at the river
and a cool wind ruffles the bluestem.
The sky is full of old bones.

ELEGY: FROM A NORTH COUNTRY JOURNAL

Mary Graham Vinz (1882-1972)

I

Almost by instinct now
the car tracks eastward through
the flat Red River Valley land
toward frozen lakes and hills.
The towns are copies of each other here,
squatting listlessly among their monuments
against the edges of the fields:
water tower, elevator, gas station,
railroad semaphore, church. . .

We have been taught
that when the ones we love are dying
we must go.
The slow deaths are the worst,
most like our own.

Nothing moves except the road.

II

She talks of death as I talk of life,
half believing, each of us an emissary
watching the other's eyes.
I hold her hand and read aloud
the letters from old friends,
filled with their own dying.
The heart machine ticks onward, implacably,
its message and her own the same:
one day is no different from the rest.

III

Once there were glaciers here.
Now only winter, and the terrible
survivor's pride. I drive
through fields of icy moonlight,
remembering her tales:

the man who froze to death
trying to unlock his front door,
drunk and warm on a night like this,
until they found him in the morning—
still on his knees
with the key in his hand.

And the others, the families
who died in snowdrifts
when their cars broke down,
the farmer who dropped through
river ice with a team and wagon. . .
whole generations disappearing
into glacial nights,
and those who survive
even the stalking blizzards,
alone in unfamiliar beds,
or driving endlessly toward first light.

"Stiff as a board," she said,
"with the key still in his hand."

IV

There is a house,
gaunt and thin as this hand I hold,
derelict for seven years—mausoleum
of mildew and shattered glass,
walls sagging together
like a child's watercolor.
Only the necessities still work:
outhouse, pump, and wood-stove.
She didn't want to leave.

"It was never very much,
but it was mine. A widow
nearly fifty years in that house,
but I provided.
Two sons,
and just my sewing money,
through the lean years
that never ended.
I've put aside enough
to bury me. See to it."

And the lean wisdom
garnered day to day:
don't count on much,
be neighborly and
mind your business.
Don't take too many baths.
It weakens you.

V

And now there is only the last visit,
there is only spring,
an alien season,
and this tiled room shrinking
to a smooth point on her forehead—
the wintry shadow that will not go away,
that will not be exorcized by light.
She waits. Her hands
creep out unaware of themselves,
slowly meticulously crocheting
with imaginary threads
a tiny rosary of the years,
a blind message
where only one thing is sure:

at last and always
I am with you
in the long sleep of your waking
in the clock that rides forever in your eye
I am with you in the windy light
when the voice of our last tear is silenced
with nothing to remember
nothing to remember us by.

Charles Waterman

THE NEW COWS

Like thunder they come out, like Holstein thunder-
these dark females swinging their heavy equipment, these
    barbarous ladies
that slip, fall, run with irregular glances
at us. No one touches them; they keep their separateness, in fear.
In a moment we can abandon our proprietary poses for the real work,
which is to get each of the hornless, black and white
blocks of female energy to a particular stall
and lock her head in it. At first,
it is like being in a mill of giants: each cow's strength,
multiples of mine, is a sea wave, against which
we skid and shout, and often just
get out of the way.
        Finally we outwit them; we
pick a particular cow, and though she bolts and shoves,
we stanchion her. One by one, cursing, exhilarated,
    we do the same
to all but one huge heifer. She has never
been in a barn before, and she won't move. We rope her;
        even then we can't hold her;
we tie her to a solid post and watch, dismayed,
as she bucks and falls and bats her head
on concrete. When she gets her wind we winch her,
one step at a time, toward food she refuses to recognize.
        Later, while they eat, we milk them;
by electric light we go among them, washing and talking,
joking and happy. Two-thirds of the way through milking,
we find a "woman" who will be tonight's favorite:
she stands on two hooves while the machine is on her,
and almost dances.

LOOKING FOR LAMBS
—for Richard and Judith Strohl

Richard has fitted me out with rainsuit
and a flashlight, so that I am dry
and can see the two hundred eighty or so shapes
in the rain like tinsel on dark trees.
Lightning will hit the silo first,
he said. As instructed, I pry over the backs of sheep
and under their bellies, looking for lambs.
The lightning! A white horse
whinnies and runs to the end of the fence!
After my coffee,
I meet a ewe with two white mats
she is guarding. Putting the light down,
I edge toward her,
grab her and walk astride her to the barn, my fingers
deep in her wool.
The cows look at us as if we were coming in drunk.
I throw her into a pen. Pinching wool from her teats
I start milk from her. Then go back for the lambs
which are where the light is lying
in its hall of rain.
I can carry them easily in one arm.
One stands and sucks; but the other...
I carry it to the house to waken Judith.
Sitting in her kitchen full of sick
and recovered lambs,
watching her work,
I think of men who have been out rescuing girls
from rivers; I look at *Newsweek*.
I think of horses who have half a lightning bolt
inside them, running. I find I have lost my hat.
By morning I think, I will need help walking home.

SPRING CHORES

Toward spring the cattle are getting lice-bald.
You knew all along they were nothing but bones and hides.
The cows have already had their annual warm-day dance.
and you have already laughed at them,
bobbing like teeter-totters, running in mud,
butting heads and mounting each other
as if the whole world were in heat!
Your mouth shuts up after that.
Winter has done terrible things to the hay,
and the silage is gone.
You need to get through April to be here in May.

If you are lucky there will be no more storms.
Every morning your children seem happier.
You go on carrying the manure out,
go on looking for the can of whizz that starts the tractor,
feed twigs and burlap sacks on watered ice.

Elizabeth Weber

KANSAS, 1920

I am a girl who stands among sheets
drying one by one in Kansas daylight.
They starch to a white beyond the simple roll
of these hills to dazzle my eyes.
In sheets like these they wrapped my brother
who yielded his body in a killing
called war, as if that made it more right.
The hole they blew in his side explodes in my head.
It stays now a place for the day to escape to.
In her grief my mother gave up his clothing,
his books, the planes he modeled from balsam,
gave them up to sky in a black furl,
as if the heat of that burning could wipe out the hurt she felt.
It wiped my brother bodily from this planet.
All that's left is a shirt I stole
and keep balled in my dresser away from my mother's hands.
My sister gives herself to every man she can
as if that could fill the hollow spot my brother left.
She says she wants to take in all their emptiness.
She looks in their eyes for a matching emptiness
where she can place herself, but finds instead an ache
like a fist.   My father says hell glories on this earth.
Nothing more. Salvation is what big men talk about
when they want something. Like a church
or my brother. Every night he carves
rounds of cottonwood into the smooth moons of napkin holders.
I call them cries without faces.
I stand here by these starching sheets and know wisdom
waits in the field with the corn.
Grow, says the sun, and it grows.
Bend, says the rain, and it bends.
Die, says the cold, and it dies.
As I bend to the weight of these sheets
I watch them die a little each day with the wash
but come glorious in the sun,
bright flags against an empty Kansas prairie.

MY GRANDMOTHER'S HANDS

In the cracked October morning
I watch my hands rim
the edge of the pail.
Numb with hard tap water
they redden as the sky does.
When did this happen, my hands
become furrowed like an old burr oak,
an afterimage of yours?

How clearly I see your slow body
thicken into the light
haloed by the hollyhocks
as you etch your way to the coop.
My fledgling hand held tight
in the sinew and bone clutch
of yours.

At five, I cluck to you
like one of the hens
you won't let me touch
for fear I'll become as marked
as you by their beaks.
You speak of yourself as a coat
ready for the junk heap,
and not that Polish daughter
I saw pictured once high on a hay rack,
the men looped around you.
Did you think you could keep
the world from flicking its knife-edged
tongue at me any more than yourself?

At thirty and alone, I'm world-bitten,
these hands you worked so hard to save
scarred as old barn wood
and dry as husks of corn
blown by September.
They do what they must do,
as yours did.
When do we learn to hate age,
to think of it not as growth
but as a falling away?
This curse notched in us so tightly
there is no forgiveness
for what is only self becoming

the self. My hair grays into a mirror
of yours. One day, I will lie down
next to you, my hand
dissolving into your hands.

THE WIND TAKING MY NAME

Each day thins in me,
the Dakota countryside stripped flat
of familiar oak and elm. The horizon pared
to an eternity of line.

Yesterday, milk vetch made the horses go mad.
They kicked down two fences,
one broke a leg and had to be shot.
Baby Ingrid hides in the closet
and won't come out since the big wind came
and took the barn.
It played god with the cattle,
picked them up, bawling
dropped them flat like bugs.

Lars and I are beyond ourselves.
We try to follow the long cord back
to you and father, to those quiet houses
pitched on the bank of the river near Mariestad
where the land held us like family,
but can't recall life past this hard plain,
where nothing grows but the wind
with no trees to catch and tame it.

I am thrown back on myself,
face and hands turned strangers.
I will die here, mother,
the wind taking my name
to hurl at the cancelled sky.
The grass will roll over me
as it rolls over all tools
left to bleach in the prairie sun.

ALL GONE

Most times, wind forgets this hill, the lilac
calm in the shade of basswood. The laundry,
limp on the line, starches in the August sun.
In the doze of noon, where sparrows
flee to the next country, a barn
dies of inertia, and roads mislay direction.
Each day I take my hoe and hack
at the long furrows with corn in between.
Each day the world gives me back my name.

Last week a neighbor ran his daughter
down with a tractor, thinking her a rock.
The night breezes carry his wails, and his wife
carries his troubles. I stare at the way
the lines in my palms tell my fate, and hope
for rain to soothe the alfalfa.

From my porch, I watch the dark
eat its way through the trees.
I watch the slow event of stars
across the sky. So must it have been
for my grandmother who left me this place
and went to the grave clinging
to my hand and a belief in eternal
happiness. No peace in her gray eyes, no
light cracked through the window
when the air rushed from her broken mouth.

I went out. The hills in the west
exploded. The fields emptied
with the cry of locusts.

Roberta Hill Whiteman

WHAT SHE NAMED HIM
—*for Darlene*

Shishaywin, Breath of God,
sleeps with ten days of new life curled
in his tight fists,
his arms still coated
with birthing down,
his left arm stretched over him
a little moan.
He peers at mother's dress,
the turquoise of a still familiar sky.
God blows up new leaves outside the window.
The willow prepares her summer whispers.

In his blanket of pink, cats and blue zebras,
he grunts and flushes,
feeling himself swimming the sea
to her arms, squinting when he feels again
the dust God blew into his eyes
as he emerged.
Our wisdom must be earth-won.

He will be an orator.
Already he raises his left arm for silence.
His face composed as a poppy.
His mouth oh-oh in astonishment
of what comes—butterfly, stone,
turtle, shoe, mushroom, star, toes.
The roaring train startles his afternoon.
Sucking four fingers at a time,
he dreams of poling a tule boat
under dense purple shadows,
the glowing reeds, an envelope
of glowing greens, indigo, soft yellow,
while the unseen breath of God
flattens cumulus, fosters
hair he'll find in another month.

What can we give him?
This new world.
White flags of strawberries
signal its coming. Already our adolescent
sun has juggled greater
configurations of stars.

Breath of God, *Shishaywin*,
smiles at the wall, then bleats
at his new world. He plans to tell jokes,
to travel south, to offer his mother

heartache and joy
at the same moment
one in each hand.

CALL ME LESS THAN ALL I AM

For ages and ages
under clear summer nights
I bridged wind and stars

See how I live
Every bit of bark, every limb and flat leaf
        explores a different span
My canopy of edges
        nourished the origins
        of your blood   your brooding

Call me a cedar growing from rocks
Call me the record of earth's blessings
Watch me curve   coil   throw a sinewy hook
then come murmur with me
Let go the rigid patterns
        of streets and submarines

My resin scents the earth
as I grope through the velvet warmth
of dirt   just beyond your reach
just in need of your touch
My creators remind me of my girth
My leaves stop stars before your eyes

When wind fills me
        the music I am
        clings to every branch
Through me   the processions of stars
the spiral dance of earth
Through me   your backbone
and your worth

What shelter without my green youth
My spirit always faces south
        and yours
Even as I creak I offer a home
        to katies that did
        to katies that didn't
        and you

118

THE EARTH AND I ARE ONE

I

Out of the layers of air,
one star whose fragrance fills the wind
                    comes dancing.
Out of the layers of air,
the sun, our brother, flies.
We are wrapped in his wings.
His golden glance hurls us spiraling
through space,
            through time,
                        through dark.

In dawn light we walk gratefully
            in a living world.
The living wind breathes us,
moves in and out,
        spins in and out, up and
through spaces in the blue,
spaces where fading stars twinkle back.

Now shadows will lengthen and grow bold.
Day unwraps his hair
and sets out on the open road.
Each day, a new vision,
    clouds and ravines,
        blue wind and buds.

II

Now grasses, blue, green
jolt us with their reach,
pushing through leafmold
    to tremble with the urgent energy
        of their soft
            bristling songs.
Grasses beguile the geese
        northward, northward.
Now let us rest in their long touch,
let their delight shimmer over us,
until we too unfurl ourselves
        through this living world.

Under a blaze of maples,
under birches shaking their catlins,
under white pine's massive buoyancy
over the white flowers, the blood red fruit

of strawberries, over these hills
       echoing buds and gusts of rain,
let us walk gratefully in this living world
          again.

III

You say there were no birds
       before this moment.
We hear their chorus and clatter
Warblers whistling in woody coverts,
phoebes in the bare tree boughs,
thrushes, finches winging brightly
       over rivers.

We walk gratefully under their passage,
grateful they've returned from
       long migrations.

Now *kli kli* chatter
       a cardinal cheeps, a chip of sun
          swinging over a knowing oak.
Above the reeds, *las kali saks*
       sings her name.
You say there were no birds
       before this moment.
Now a nuthatch scales the pine
with needles in her beak,
grateful for this living world.

Within this whirling
a hawk scans the river, fish feed
ripples to the light,
squirrels melt into tree boles,
bears thicken the woods with their growls.
Only the deer's spoor remains.
       They dreamed us with their hunger.
       They sustain us with their love.

IV

Under the spring moon
peepers begin.
       Their rhythms rising through layers
of green reflections add up the heartbeats
of our childhood. When water's great-throated
bulbous children, marked with crosses,
ripen Spring, birds dare not chirp.

Because of their ringing,
stars flicker and dim, flicker,
begin without weariness.
Because of their ringing,
the wind flutters her scarves
through the swamp. Her scarves, like foolish
fires, leap from hollow to hill,
as she hurries over the ridge
under this living moon.

SHELTERBELT AT LAKEVIEW

Slivers of green
sang in the haze that March morning
hired men came to plow.
Sunlight dappled cottonwood trunks.
Dew sparkled in deer-downed grass.
The whole half-mile of trees
broke to early budding
as she passed tractors
grinding dry flats.

She walked the shelterbelt to work.
A tenant without rights
to the life of those trees,
she welcomed
wind racing up each slope,
jostling every branch,
until the whole windbreak
surged with more life
than she could muster.

All day
hired men plowed and stacked
and worked the earth,
churned clods of dirt from dangling roots,
left buds to wither on each bough
while a whirlwind of swallows
twisted toward less furrowed fields.

"Now," they chimed,
"our irrigators can turn."

That evening she walked
a mud-drubbed road.
A moraine of spines dried to tinder.
Ripped from their centers,
the cottonwoods sifted their remaining songs.
Like hourglasses left askew,
they measured mortal breath.

Because wood healed her blood
for generations, all the long
clear nights, she lay listening
to their soughing, listening to water
receding from the hard, brilliant sky.

Then one dawn
she heard hawks screaming
as they settled on blackened boughs.

She's gone to meet
their fierce gaze,
soughing as she steps
through the lost treeline.
She's never forgotten
how air fretted over those acres.

See them now,
trunks not yet buried by the plow,
eleven hawks spiraling
from precarious perches,
one after another,
keeping their heavy wings
hooked on the dawning air,
sweeping over lakebeds lost
a generation ago?

She wanted us to know
their eyes austere,
their austere rising
guards a wedge of silence
longer than any lack of rain,
stronger than this coming storm.

Contributors

Joseph Amato is a Professor of History and Director of Rural Studies at Southwest State University in Marshall, Minnesota. He is the author of *Countryside, Mirror of Ourselves*; *Ethics, Living or Dead*; *Death Book: Terrors, Consolations, Contradictions & Paradoxes*; *Guilt and Gratitude, A Study of the Origins of Contemporary Conscience*; *Suffering, A Theory of Value*; and *When Father and Son Conspire, A Study of A Minnesota Farm Murder*.

Wendell Berry lives and farms with his family in Kentucky. Among his many books are: *Collected Poems: 1957-1982*; the novels *A Place on Earth* and *Nathan Coulter*; a collection of stories, *The Wild Birds*; and three collections of essays, *Recollected Essays: 1965-1980*, *The Gift of Good Land: Further Essays Cultural and Agricultural*, and *Standing by Words*, all from North Point Press.

Robert Bly was born and raised in Madison, MN (forty-eight miles north of Marshall, MN) and after leaving for the Navy, Harvard, New York, Iowa City, and Norway, returned to the family farm in 1958 to live and write. His *Silence in the Snowy Fields* (Wesleyan University Press, 1962)—from which three poems are reprinted here—is now in its 11th printing. *Selected Poems* appeared in 1986 (Harper and Row), along with *The Winged Life: The Poetic Voice of Henry David Thoreau* (Sierra Club Books). He currently lives and writes in Moose Lake, MN.

William Boggs was born in Erie, Pennsylvania, and raised in a remote rural area of northwest Pennsylvania. He earned a Doctor of Arts degree in creative writing from Carnegie-Mellon University and currently teaches at Robert Morris College. A collection of his poems, *Swimming in Clear Water*, is forthcoming from Barnwood Press.

Robert L. Carothers was born and raised in rural western Pennsylvania. He served as President of Southwest State University, Marshall, MN, from 1983-1986, and is currently Chancellor of the State University System of Minnesota. His books include *Poems for the End of Something* (1969), *Freedom and Other Times* (The Poet's Press, 1972), and *John Calvin's Favorite Son* (Barnwood Press, 1980). He lives in Lake Forest, Minnesota.

Amy Clampitt was born and brought up in rural Iowa and graduated from Grinnell College. Since then, she has lived mainly in New York City, earning a living in and around book publishing. Her full-length collections of poems are: *The Kingfisher* (Knopf, 1983), *What the Light Was Like* (Knopf, 1985), and *Archaic Figure* (Knopf, 1987). She also has been a Guggenheim Fellow (1982-3), Visiting Writer at Amherst College (1986-7), Phi Beta Kappa Poet at the Harvard University Literary Exercises (1987), and was elected to the American Academy of Arts and Letters in 1987.

Philip Dacey is professor of English at Southwest State University and the Director of the Marshall Festival. His most recent books of poems include *The Man with Red Suspenders* (Milkweed Editions, 1986) and *Strong Measures: Contemporary American Poetry in Traditional Forms* (co-edited with David Jauss, Harper & Row, 1985). During the Spring of 1988, he was a Fulbright Writer-in-Residence in Yugoslavia.

Leo Dangel lives in Marshall, Minnesota, and teaches English at Southwest State University. His book, *Old Man Brunner Country*, was published by Spoon River Poetry Press, 1987.

Dave Etter has published eighteen books of poetry, the latest being *Live at the Silver Dollar* and *Selected Poems*, both from Spoon River Poetry Press, and his *Midlanders* is due out in 1988. His *Alliance, Illinois* has been adapted for the stage by three different theater groups. He lives in Elburn, Illinois (pop. 1200) with his wife and two children.

David Allan Evans was born and raised in Sioux City, Iowa, earned his MA from the University of Iowa, and his MFA from the University of Arkansas, and currently teaches in the English Department at South Dakota State University in Brookings. His books of poetry include *Real and False Alarms* (Bk Mk Press, 1985), *Train Windows* (Ohio University Press, 1976), and a collection of essays, *Remembering the Soos* (Plains Press, 1986).

Linda M. Hasselstrom is a rancher in western South Dakota who operated from 1971 to 1985 Independent Publishing Services, publishing works of poetry, fiction, and non-fiction associated with the Great Plains. She is the author of two books of poetry, *Caught on the Wing* (Julie Holcomb Letterpress, 1984) and *Roadkill* (Spoon River Poetry Press, 1987); two books of nonfiction, *Windbreak: A Woman Rancher on the Northern Plains* (Barn Owl Books, 1987) and *Going Over East: Reflections of a Woman Rancher* (Winner of the 1987 American Writing Award from Fulcrum, Golden, Colorado, 1987; and the editor of *Journal of a Mountain Man: James Clyman* (Mountain Press, 1984) and *Horizons: The South Dakota Writers' Anthology* (Lame Johnny Press, 1984).

Tom Hennen has two children and has worked for the Minnesota Department of Natural Resources since 1974. His books of poems include *The Heron with No Business Sense* (1974), *The Hole in the Landscape Is Real* (1976), *Selected Poems, 1963-1983* (1983), and *Looking into the Weather* (1983).

Jim Heynen was born on a farm near Sioux Center, Iowa, the second son of first generation Dutch-American parents. He was educated at the Universities of Oregon and Iowa, and lived in South Dakota. Jim Heynen's poetry, fiction, and nonfiction have appeared in many newspapers and periodicals, and his most recent books include *The*

Man who Kept Cigars in his Cap (stories, 1979, now in its third printing); *A Suitable Church* (poems, 1981); and *You Know What is Right* (stories, 1985) which received the Pacific Northwest Booksellers' Award for books published that year. He was also a contributing writer to *City of Dreams*, (nonfiction, 1986), an encyclopedic documentation of Washington's Olympic Peninsula.

Bill Holm is from Minneota, Minnesota, the grandson of Icelandic immigrant farmers. He has been a Fulbright lecturer in American Literature at the University of Iceland in Reykjavik, received fellowships from the Bush Foundation and National Endowment for the Arts, and after a year's teaching in central China, currently teaches in the English Department at Southwest State University. His recent books include *Boxelder Bug Variations* (prose, poetry, and music) from Milkweed Editions, and a collection of essays, *The Music of Failure* (Plains Press, 1985), which has been reissued in an expanded cloth edition, *Prairie Days*, by Saybrook Publishers (1987).

Greg Keeler lives in Bozeman, Montana, with his wife, Judy, and his boys, Chris and Max. He teaches in the English Department at Montana State University and has published three collections of poems through Confluence Press: *Spring Catch, The Far Bank*, and *American Falls*. Three of his tapes of satirical ballads are available through Earth First! Music: *Songs of Fishing, Sheep and Guns in Montana; Talking Sweet Bye and Bye;* and *Bad Science Fiction*.

Michael Kincaid has been publishing poems in literary magazines since 1967, the year he started one of the first public poetry reading series in Minneapolis. In 1973 a book of poems, *To Walk in the Daylight*, was independently published in a limited edition. In 1985, another limited edition, *Cave Light*, was published. Since Winter 1985, his essay-column *Notes of a Wolf Shepherd* has been a regular feature of *Milkweed Chronicle*.

William Kloefkorn lives in Lincoln, Nebraska, where he teaches in the English Department at Nebraska Wesleyan University. He has several collections of poetry, the most recent being *Houses and Beyond* and *A Life Like Mine*. Another is forthcoming from Dooryard Press, *Learning It*, and another, *Drinking the Tin Cup Dry*, is in process. He is married to Eloise. They have four children, two girls and two boys, and five grandchildren. His hobbies are kite-flying, whittling, and hog-calling.

Ted Kooser is the author of many collections of poems, among them *Sure Signs* and *One World at A Time* (both from the University of Pittsburgh Press), and most recently, *The Blizzard Voices*, from Bieler Press. He lives in the country near Garland, Nebraska, and makes his living as an insurance executive.

Thomas McGrath, born and raised on a farm near Sheldon, North Dakota, has received many awards in his long and distinguished career, including a Rhodes scholarship, an Amy Lowell Traveling Scholarship, and Guggenheim, Bush, and National Endowment for the Arts Poetry and Senior Fellowships. Among his many volumes of poetry are *The Movie at the End of the World: Collected Poems*, *Passages Toward the Dark* (Collected Poems, Volume II), *Echoes Inside the Labyrinth*, and the four books of *Letter to An Imaginary Friend*. He has also published two novels, two books for children, and numerous film scripts. Retired from Moorhead State University, he lives in Minneapolis.

Before retirement, **Don Olsen** was a librarian at Southwest State University. He started the Ox Head Press in 1966.

Joe Paddock has worked in such jobs as Community Poet for the town of Olivia, Minnesota; Regional Poet for the Southwest Minnesota Arts and Humanities Council; Poet-in-Residence for Minnesota Public Radio; and Humanist-in-Residence for the American Farm Project of the National Farmers Union and for the Land Stewardship Project. His books of poetry include *Stored Light* and *A Song Like My Own* (Southwest MN Arts and Humanities Council), *Handful of Thunder* (Anvil Press), and *Earth Tongues* (Milkweed Editions). He is also the principal author of *Soil and Survival* (Sierra Club Books, 1986).

Nancy Paddock is co-author, with Joe Paddock and Carol Bly, of *Soil and Survival: Land Stewardship and the Future of American Agriculture* (Sierra Club, 1986); she also edits *The Land Stewardship Newsletter* and is the author of a one-act play, *Planting in the Dust*. Her books of poems include *Across the Full River* (1977) and *Why I Feed the Birds* (1978), both published by the Southwest Minnesota Arts and Humanities Council, and *A Dark Light* (Vanilla Press, 1978). Currently, she works for the COMPAS Writers-in-the-Schools and Dialogue programs.

David Pichaske's books include a poetry textbook anthology, *Beowulf to Beatles* (Macmillan, 1981); literary criticism, *Chaucer's Literary Pilgrimage* (Norwood, 1977); social criticism, *A Generation in Motion: Popular Music and Culture in the '60s* (Schirmer, 1979); popular music criticism, *The Poetry of Rock* (Ellis Press, 1981); non-fiction, *The Jubilee Diary, April 10, 1980-April 19, 1981*, and a chapbook of poems, *Visiting the Father* (Dacotah Territory, 1987). He is publisher-editor of Spoon River Poetry Press and Chair of the English Department at Southwest State University.

John Rezmerski is the author of *Held for Questioning* (University of Missouri Press, 1969), *An American Gallery* (Three Rivers Press, 1977), *Dreams of Bela Lugosi* (Knife River Press, 1979), and *Growing Down* (Minnesota Writers' Publishing House/Westerheim Press, 1982). He teaches poetry, science fiction, and journalism at Gustavus Adolphus College, besides doing free-lance writing and editing.

Barton Sutter was raised in small towns in Minnesota and Iowa. His first collection, *Cedarhome*, was published by BOA Editions in 1977, and his chapbook, *Sequoyah*, was issued by the Ox Head Press in 1983. *Pine Creek Parish Hall and Other Poems*, published by the Sandhills Press in 1986, was awarded the Bassine Citation by The Academy of American Poets. For ten years Sutter earned his living as a typesetter, working for commercial shops in Minneapolis and Boston. More recently, he has been teaching at Saint John's University and the University of Minnesota. He lives in Duluth with his wife, historian Annette Atkins.

Thom Tammaro was born and raised in the steel valley of western Pennsylvania, and has lived in the Midwest for the past fifteen years. Currently, he lives in Moorhead, MN, where he teaches writing and humanities at Moorhead State University. He has edited *Roving Across Fields: A Conversation and Uncollected Poems By William Stafford* (Barnwood Press, 1983) and is the author of a collection of poems, *Minnesota Suite* (Spoon River Poetry Press, 1987).

Mark Vinz was born in North Dakota, grew up in Minnesota and Kansas, and since 1968 has taught in the English Department of Moorhead State University. He is the founder and editor of the poetry journal *Dacotah Territory* (1971-81) and the Territorial Press; his most recent books of poems include *Climbing the Stairs* (Spoon River Poetry Press, 1983) *The Weird Kid* (New Rivers Press, 1983), and, forthcoming, *Minnesota Gothic* (Barnwood Press).

Charles Waterman was born in McCook, Nebraska, grew up in Colorado and Iowa, and received his BA and MA from the University of Iowa. He also did graduate study at the University of Denver, where he worked for publisher Alan Swallow and was editor of Verb Publications. His books of poetry include *Talking Animals* (Juniper Press) and *The Place* (Minnesota Writers' Publishing House). He has held a Bush Foundation Fellowship (1980-81) and since 1982 has been working primarily in visual arts, with several exhibitions in southern Minnesota.

Elizabeth Weber was born in St. Paul, Minnesota, earned an MFA from the University of Montana, and is currently working on a Ph.D. and teaching at SUNY Binghamton. She is the author of a book of poems, *Small Mercies* (Owl Creek Press) and has published work in several magazines.

Roberta Hill Whiteman teaches at the University of Wisconsin-Eau Claire. Her work has appeared in magazines and anthologies—most recently in *The Chariton Review, Early Ripening* (London: Pandora Press, edited by Marge Piercy), and *Harper's Book of Twentieth Century Native American Poetry* (edited by Duane Niatum). Her first collection of poems, *Star Quilt*, (Holy Cow! Press) won an award from the Council for Wisconsin Writers. She is currently working on her second collection.

Acknowledgements

Any effort such as this is never the work of just one or two people, so we would like to thank all those involved in the cooperative spirit of making this anthology: Vicki Kirkhorn, for typing the manuscript; Jan Guida at the Moorhead State Print Shop; Moorhead State University President Roland Dille, for his continuing support; Sheila Coghill, Tom Koontz, and David Pichaske for their assistance in preparing the manuscript; Katie Vinz, for her keen eye in proofreading the manuscript; and to all the poets, for their patience and cooperation.

All efforts were made to secure permissions from authors and publishers of these poems. Any oversights are purely unintentional. The editors extend their thanks to these publishers as well as to all the writers and publishers for their cooperation in securing reprint rights.

Joseph Amato:
"Bror Anderson's Birds" and "A Winter Peace Dance" from *Death Book* (Venti Amati) ©1985. Reprinted with permission of the author.

Wendell Berry:
"The Peace of Wild Things," "The Man Born to Farming," "To What Listens," and "The Wild Geese" reprinted from *Collected Poems, 1957-1982*, copyright ©1985 by Wendell Berry. Published by North Point Press and reprinted by permission. All rights reserved.

Robert Bly:
"Driving Toward the Lac Qui Parle River," "Laziness and Silence," and "Snowfall in the Afternoon" are from *Silence in the Snowy Fields* (Wesleyan University Press, 1962), copyright ©1962 by Robert Bly and reprinted with his permission; "Sitting with My Mother and Father," "My Father at 85," and "The Potato" Robert Bly and reprinted with his permission.

William Boggs:
"Morning" first appeared in *Nightsun*; "Country Town Love Story" and "Red Tail," ©1987 by William Boggs. Reprinted with permission of the author.

Robert L. Carothers:
"Muskrat," "Charlie No-Face," ©1972 Robert L. Carothers. Reprinted from *Freedom and Other Times* with permission from The Poet's Press. "Hunt Poem" ©1973 by Robert L. Carothers and "My Brother," ©1980 by Robert L. Carothers. From *John Calvin's Favorite Son* by Robert L. Carothers. Reprinted by permission of The Barnwood Press and the author.

Amy Clampitt:
"Witness," from *What the Light was Like* (Alfred A. Knopf), copyright ©1985 by Amy Clampitt and used with her permission. "The Arrow in My Mind" first appeared in *River Styx*, No. 14 (1984). Reprinted with permission of the author.

Mark Vinz:
"Elegy: from a North Country Journal" first appeared in *South Dakota Review* (Autumn 1976); "Lost and Found" first appeared in *The Spoon River Quarterly* (Fall, 1984); "Homesteaders" first appeared in the *North Dakota Quarterly* (Fall 1985); "Midcontinent" and "In A Drought Year" are from *Climbing the Stairs* (Spoon River Poetry Press) ©1983 by Mark Vinz. Reprinted with permission of the author.

Charles Waterman:
"The New Cows" and "Spring Chores" reprinted from *The Place* (Minnesota Writers' Publishing House) ©1977 by Charles Waterman; "Looking for Lambs" reprinted from *Talking Animals*. Reprinted with permission of the author.

Elizabeth Weber:
"My Grandmother's Hands" first appeared in *Women and Aging: An Anthology, Calyx: A Journal of Art and Literature by Women*. Vol 9, #2 #3. Winter 1986. "All Gone" and "The Wind Taking My Name" first appeared in *Calyx: A Journal of Art and Literature by Women*. Vol. 7, #3, Winter 1984. Reprinted with permission of the author and publisher. "Kansas, 1920" first appeared in *Graham House Review*, Fall 1985. Reprinted with permission of the publisher. "All Gone" and "The Wind Taking My Name" also appeared in the chapbook *Small Mercies* (Owl Creek Press, 1984). Reprinted with permission of the author and publisher.

Roberta Hill Whiteman:
"Shelterbelt at Lakeview," "What She Named Him," "Call Me Less Than All I Am," and "The Earth and I Are One" copyright ©1987 by Roberta Hill Whiteman. Reprinted with permission of the author.